Ludwig Merkle

Sissi

The Tragic Empress

The Story of Elisabeth of Austria

Bruckmann

Title: Empress Elisabeth in Hungarian coronation regalia,
painted in 1867 by Georg Raab (detail, see also page 63).

Page 1: Sisi, painted by the Hungarian Gyula Benczúr,
a professor at the Academy in Munich.

Page 2/3: Coursing in Silesia. In the centre, on a white
horse, Empress Elisabeth.

Page 4/5: Laxenburg Castle, to the south of Vienna, where
Sisi spent her lonely honeymoon.

Page 6/7: Now carefully renovated, Possenhofen Castle is
today the home of a select few.

Page 8/9: The young Empress's first escape was in 1860 –
to the Atlantic island of Madeira.

Page 10/11: The Imperial Castle of Schönbrunn, the most
popular tourist sight in Vienna.

Cover design: Uwe Richter
Edited by Dr Sabine Klinkert
Layout: Bettina Schippel

English translation: Ingrid Taylor, Munich

Printed on paper treated with low-clorine bleach.

Die Deutsche Bibliothek – CIP data

Sissi : the tragic empress : the story of Elisabeth of
Austria / Ludwig Merkle. – München : Bruckmann, 1996
Dt. Ausg. u.d.T.: Sissi
ISBN 3-7654-2857-4
NE: Merkle, Ludwig

Contents

Preface: Everybody Knows Sisi

She is – so they say, and perhaps they may even be right – the most popular of all Austrian women, and the best known internationally. Posterity still likes to remember her. Almost everybody who has ever visited the cinema has seen at least one Sissi film and knows:

That Sisi was a Bavarian princess.

That Sisi married the Austrian Emperor Franz Josef, in fact for love.

That Sisi was sweet.

That Sisi was the most beautiful woman in the world.

She had a wicked mother-in-law.

That Sisi was a close friend of King Ludwig II of Bavaria.

And that in the end she was murdered.

It is less well known that she wrote her name with only one "s": "Sisi", not "Sissi"; "Sissi" was her name in the film. (But our book title is still spelled "Sissi" because "Sisi" appears a little disconcerting, while the form with the double "s" looks much more familiar).

She had no great achievements to her credit. And even the humbler, traditional tasks properly expected of the consort of a King and Emperor – representing him, caring for her family, acting as the gracious mother of her country, toiling busily for social welfare, charity, health and the sick, patronising the arts – she avoided whenever possible. By rejecting everything she created her own role, as a tragic, afflicted, tearful Lady of Sorrows.

"I know very well", wrote her faithful lady-in-waiting, Countess Sztáray, "that the Empress was a legendary figure in her own lifetime. Far beyond the level of ordinary people, high above everyday life, she went her own way like a phenomenon, drawing all eyes to her."

Eulogistic court biographers told the people: "As a loving wife Elisabeth naturally shared the cares and sorrows of her Imperial consort and always regarded it as her duty to support him with her love and comfort, so as to lessen the bitterness of the cup of sorrows fate had so brutally forced upon him." (A. de Burgh, 1901). This was, of course, far from the mark, but at least it sounds much more touching and nicer than this:

She escaped from the court, from the Emperor, from the people, from her children, withdrawing into illnesses and cures, fits of weeping, exaltation, and isolation. She lived stubbornly for her beauty, her slender figure, for poetry and for her riding. She experienced disappointments, clung determinedly to her contrariness and her refusal to adapt; she knew melancholy and boredom; she cherished her freedom and her privacy. She was a woman who would not fit in, who ignored her duties, who did not want to be an Empress – but who exploited all the privileges of her Imperial dignity without any inhibition whatsoever. And still she

In the years 1864 and 1865 the famous portraitist Franz Xaver Winterhalter painted the Empress three times (see also pages 47 and 49). This picture, showing Sisi with her hair loose, was Franz Josef's favourite; it hung in his study.

The Empress wrote her name with a single "s", as can be seen from her signature. The Emperor also called her "Sisi" or "My heart's Sisi". The people honoured and admired her under the pseudonym "Sissi" or even "Sissy".

did not find happiness. Quite the opposite: "The glittering diadem of the late Princess", as the biographer and Imperial Inspector of Schools, Leo Smolle, lamented in 1904, "was not always interwoven with the roses of pleasure; far, far more often was the royal crown entwined with the thorns of bitter distress of soul."

Complete or partial failure to live up to the expectations of others is often due to either incapacity or reluctance. If to both, matters become especially awkward.

She is supposed to have said once, that "Things would have gone very badly for me in life if I hadn't become an Empress". But things went pretty badly for her anyway, even as an Empress.

Sisi's father Max was often quoted as saying, in his broad Bavarian dialect, "If we hadn't been royal, we'd have been trick riders." – This would certainly have been a more suitable job for Elisabeth.

In the court of his Munich palace (Ludwigstrasse 13), demolished in 1937, Sisi's father built a hippodrome in which he liked to appear on horseback.

The sixteen-year-old Princess Sisi on horseback in Possenhofen. This picture, painted by the history painter Karl von Piloty, was presented to Franz Josef at Christmas 1853, the year he became engaged to Sisi.

LOUISE
Herzogin in Bayern.

Possenhofen Castle on Lake Starnberg was the summer residence of the ducal family. This is where Sisi passed her childhood. From the outside the castle looks almost the same as it did then (see page 6/7); in those days, however, the park was bigger and the lakeside reserved for the family.

Duchess Ludovika (1808–1892), also called "Louise" by her family, with her two eldest children, Ludwig (born 1831), Helene (1834) and, in the cot, the newly-born Elisabeth.

Sisi, Nené, Gackl, Mapperl, Gamperl at Possi

Possenhofen Castle was built in the year 1536, 30 kilometres southwest of Munich, on the western shore of Lake Starnberg. It changed hands several times, and in 1834 it was bought, for 145,000 gulden, by Duke Max in Bavaria ("in Bavaria", a title junior to "of Bavaria"). He had it renovated and decorated and moved in with his wife and children. "The house is simple, but well run", thought Countess Festetics, "clean and neat; the cooking is good. I did not find it ostentatious; everything is agreeably old-fashioned, but refined." More spiteful Viennese ladies-in-waiting called it "beggarly".

In the 1920s the castle became a children's home; during the Second World War a rest home for mothers, and then a military hospital. In 1948 it was left to the Free State of Bavaria, which used it for housing refugees and in 1951 sold it to the private sector. It was then to become a health resort, a hotel, a beauty farm, and a telecommunications school before degenerating into a motorcycle workshop and coming down further and further in the world until it was finally rehabilitated and whitewashed, and was divided up in

1984 into 27 private flats costing millions of marks. Today the residents at the modestly understated address "Karl-Theodor-Strasse 14. 82343 Possenhofen" are fashionable people, or wealthy at the very least.

The four massive crenellated corner towers, the view over the lake unobstructed by building and the park surrounded by hedges of beech and arbor vitae, by walls, bushes and wire netting, lend it an air of beauty and exclusivity. The inquisitive public may walk around the outside and look at it closely from the north side; they may feel moved to take photographs, but to their great sorrow they are not allowed in, and they are reduced to interrogating local passers-by:

"Is this the castle where Sissi lived?" "Yes".

"And King Ludwig was here as well?" "Yes, visiting."

"Is there a museum inside?" "Naah."

"Or a pub?" "Naah."

"Can't we even go into the chapel?" "Naah, not there neither."

"Did it always look like that?" "Yes".

At least from the outside, as it is classified as a historical monument. Just that the park was considerably larger in ducal times, and stretched down to the lake, where there is now a bathing beach for the common people. Once, some years ago, a plaque stood there bearing the information that this was the birthplace of Sisi, "whose striking and almost unearthly beauty and elegance have never been forgotten". When one day the people in the castle discovered that she hadn't been born there at all, they were overcome with shame and removed the plaque.

It was in Munich that Sisi first saw the light of day, on 24th December 1837, at 10:43 a.m.; Possenhofen would have been far too cold for giving birth.

Sisi was not only a Christmas child, she

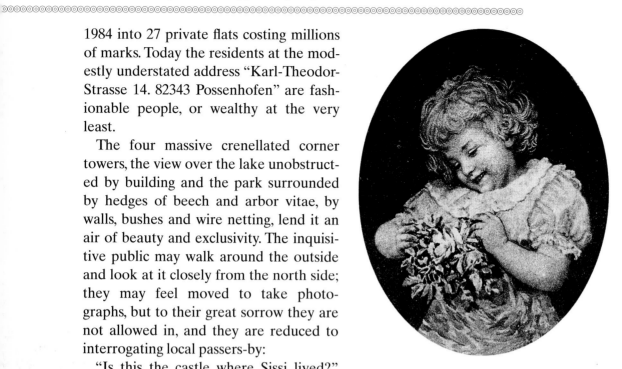

was a Sunday's child as well – a combination which looks highly promising but amounts to nothing much in the end, as we shall see.

Her mother Ludovika (1808–1892) was a half-sister of King Ludwig I of Bavaria. Well-intentioned representatives of the first generation of Sisi's biographers report: "On 9th September 1828 she followed the promptings of her heart, and married the head of the junior branch of the Wittelsbach family: Maximilian, Duke in Bavaria." (J. de la Faye). And they assert: "In her shared life with her popular but restless spouse, with whom she lived in conjugal felicity, she always maintained her evenness of temper." (C. Tschudi) and, "Although they differed in character and cast of mind the two spouses vied with each other in love and devotion and in their endeavours to make each other happy." (L. Smolle).

This is kind, but totally false. It was not her heart's promptings that Ludovika followed – she would much have preferred the Prince of Braganza – but the Wittelsbach family dictates. The marriage had al-

Lake Starnberg, with its 57 square kilometres of surface area, is Bavaria's second largest lake (after Chiemsee). Situated to the south-west of Munich it is surrounded by gentle hills and friendly village communities. Many well-known people live around here. At weekends in summer hordes of sailors and bathers descend on the lake.

ready been arranged when Max and Ludovika were small children. Recent historians have discovered that "the couple's marriage was unhappy from the outset." (B. Hamann). Ludovika sat embittered in Possenhofen Castle, fussed over her dogs, raged against fate, and suffered from migraines. As a young woman she is said to have been a "Junoesque beauty", but soon looked careworn, like Dürer's mother.

Nonetheless, her marriage produced nine children:

Ludwig (1831–1920), who became an officer and contracted a morganatic marriage completely below his station in life with a Jewish actress.

Wilhelm, born and died 1832.

Helene (1834–1890), who married the hereditary prince Maximilian von Thurn und Taxis.

Elisabeth (1837–1898).

Carl Theodor (1839–1909), "the most important, although not one of the handsomest" (Conte Corti), who became a well-known ophthalmologist.

Marie (1841–1925), most unhappily married to King Francis II of Naples.

Mathilde (1843–1925), who married the brother of the above, Count Louis of Trani.

Sophie (1847–1897), who was briefly engaged to King Ludwig II and who then married Duke Ferdinand of Alençon.

Max Emanuel (1849–1893), an officer, "strikingly handsome, but not overbright."

Possenhofen was where Sisi spent the summers of her youth; here she grew up, rather wild, and close to nature. Barefooted, not too much burdened with the riches of education and careless of court ceremonial, she played with the local peasant children, swam, rode, and spoke a broad Bavarian dialect. "The great park and the surrounding woods were the first playgrounds of this child of the open air, who grew so finely in body and whose receptive soul bore the first deep impressions of the power of Divine Nature", as we learn from Clara Tschudi in her biog-

Sisi's mother, Ludovika. She was the youngest daughter of Bavaria's King, Max I Josef, and rather unhappily married to her cousin, Duke Max in Bavaria. Nevertheless she had many children. However, she preferred the company of her dogs to that of her husband.

Duke Max in Bavaria (1808–1888), Sisi's father, was a very jolly man who enjoyed company and was an avid player of the zither. His title was Duke "in Bavaria" in contrast to the members of the older, more important line of the Dukes "of Bavaria".

Nilfahrt-Walzer.

Johann Petzmayer.

On his trip to the Orient in 1838 Duke Max took along his zither player, Johann Petzmayer, who composed a pretty "Nile Waltz" for him. Sadly this composer sank into unearned oblivion; not even the Egyptian tourist organisations have his works played.

raphy of 1906. "And the inhabitants of the Bavarian Alps still relate how 'Liese of Possenhofen' clambered over the untrodden mountain paths, finally emerging with armfuls of edelweiss". Which is also untrue, unfortunately; there are indeed some low hills around Possenhofen (up to 728 m above sea-level), but nothing remotely resembling a mountain where anybody, even a princess, could pick edelweiss.

"Liese of Possenhofen"'s full Christian names were Elisabeth Amalie Eugenie; she was known as "Sisi". The ducal family at Possenhofen was very fond of affectionate nicknames: Helene was called "Nené", Carl Theodor "Gackl", Max Emanuel "Mapperl". The castle was "Possi", and Mother Ludovika "Mimi". Their father was given no such display of affection; he was not home often enough. With an annual appanage of 250,000 gulden and – despite his rank as Bavarian major-general and the "Royal Highness" granted him in 1845 – without any tiresome duties, he followed his inclinations, rode,

And here he is our Duke Max again, playing his zither. The rower in this picturesque group is Emperor Franz Josef, and of course, the lady is Sisi. The scene is supposed to be Lake Starnberg; behind the Emperor we can see Possenhofen Castle.

This is Nené/Helene, the first choice of the wise mother of the Emperor, but Franz Josef wanted her sister Sisi. Well, it was his own fault, then, we can say. Nené consoled herself with a prince from the House of Thurn und Taxis.

hunted, wrote poetry and composed, held many convivial gatherings with the poets, musicians and scholars who were his friends, was liberal and popular, maintained a private circus in the court of his palace in Munich, fraternised affably with citizens, peasants and also peasant women, collected folk-songs, played the zither, sang merry Alpine ditties to its accompaniment, and travelled abroad.

When his daughter Sisi was four weeks old he set out on an eight-month journey to the Orient. His retinue included his court chamber virtuoso on the zither, Johann Petzmayer, who took his revenge by writing a "Nile Voyage Waltz" in Egypt. "The wild native tribes", so the tradition has it, "listened with delight to his zither playing." This conjures up a vivid picture. The duke also brought back four Moorish boys he had bought at a slave-market in Cairo, and had them baptised by the Archbishop in the Frauenkirche, to the great interest of the people of Munich.

We have conflicting reports of his virtues as a father. Thus, we learn that he was very popular with his children and that Sisi was his favourite daughter; but also that the relationship between the two was "never good at any time in his life."

As Empress, Sisi often returned to Lake Starnberg. In those days she would stay, with a retinue fifty strong, in Feldafing, in the "Hotel Strauch", which is almost exactly 1550 metres from the Castle. From the local guide to Feldafing we learn that: "For her morning toilette soft lake-water was provided for her, which the fish-buyer Andreas Vitzthum had to bring for her daily in a jug from Possenhofen." The hotel is now called "Empress Elisabeth", and honours its exalted guest with a white memorial in the park by the tennis-court, and by the "Empress" menu which the chef prepares on suitable occasions.

Love Like a Flash of Lightning

Bad Ischl is still styled "the tiny old Imperial town in the heart of the Salzkammergut." The Austrian Imperial family had stayed here for the summer since the 1820s. Franz Josef spent sixty summers of his life, or even eighty-three – the figures vary – in Ischl.

And this is also where the Imperial marriage with Princess Sisi was made.

In fact Franz Josef's mother, the Archduchess Sophie, had actually intended her son to marry Helene, Sisi's older sister. So that they could see each other and become more closely acquainted, the Emperor arrived at Ischl with his mother, retinue and relations on 16th August 1853 to meet Mother Ludovika with her

Following double page:

Here we see the young bridal couple on their first outing together to the Salzkammergut, riding in a comfortable coach drawn by six horses. It can hardly have been an intimate occasion, for a huge entourage was trotting along behind.

The young bridegroom, fashionably attired and as yet without the full beard, and the girl Sisi, aged 15 and three-quarters, shown here on a picture painted on porcelain. Franz Josef was 23 and had been Austrian Emperor for five years. The engagement at Ischl had been the most romantic deed in his life.

daughter Helene from Possenhofen. And Sisi was there, too, for no particular reason, she just happened to be there.

But then the programme collapsed.

"As the carriage rolled along the dusty country road Franz Josef caught sight of a wonderfully beautiful young girl playing with a herd of goats in a field. The next moment the carriage rounded a corner and approached the spa of Ischl. An hour later, as the Emperor sat with his mother, a young girl rushed unannounced into the drawing room, a bunch of wild roses in her hand." (E. M. Kronfeld)

Or were there really any goats? Perhaps the Emperor met "a child in the deep shadows of the park-like wood; she had on a short white dress, and her wonderful mass of wavy, silky chestnut-brown hair fell around her slender girlish form to her tiny feet. Two hounds were prancing about her."? (M. Cuncliffe Owen)

Or did the adjutant see the child first? And "suddenly let out a cry of admiration. 'Look there, your Majesty!' he exclaimed. Franz Josef pulled out his field-glass." (C. Tschudi).

Perhaps, however, the Emperor was walking quite alone, lost in thought, when suddenly he stopped and listened. "A girl's voice was singing : 'God Preserve the Emperor Franz, the Emperor, our good Emperor Franz.' Franz Josef slipped behind a tree to observe the singer from this hiding-place. He saw a childlike, slender girlish form pass by, happy and carefree. She was wearing a wide-brimmed straw hat trimmed with wild flowers and had fluttering red velvet ribbons on her arm; she sang over and over again, 'God Preserve the Emperor Franz, the Emperor, our good Emperor Franz.' [It must be pointed out here that this was the National Anthem of Austria.]

Ischl (officially designated a spa since 1906) is Austria's oldest salt water spa resort; it helps people with rheumatism and heart, circulatory, breathing and disc problems. In the appropriately decorated Imperial "Betrothal Rooms" quite ordinary couples can celebrate "Sisi weddings". In the foreground is the "Emperor's Villa".

Then Franz Josef emerged from his hiding-place and doffed his hat in greeting [...] Franz Josef gazed intently into the girl's face, so fine and pretty as a picture, in which a pair of great dark-blue eyes shone." (M. Blank-Eismann).

The girl, of course, was Princess Sisi, and the ill-starred encounter actually took place, quite plainly and simply, over tea at the Villa Eltz, otherwise known as the Emperor's villa. Apart from that, Sisi

was not wearing a short, white dress but a black one, and her eyes were light brown. But it is true that they were attracted to each other. Franz Josef found Sisi far more appealing than Helene, who had been intended for him, and just two days later he reached his decision; she was the one he would marry. "Above the political clouds which had darkened the first years of his reign love flashed down into his heart like a streak of lightning."

The "Emperor's Villa" was a wedding present from the Emperor's mother, Sophie. She had two extra wings built on, which made the ground plan into an "E" shape, E for Elisabeth. In addition to the antlers of many animals shot dead by the Emperor, the villa also contains original furniture, pictures, Sisi's riding crop, fans, death masks etc. and even Franz Josef's leather breeches.

(C. Tschudi) On 18th August 1853, the Emperor's 23rd birthday, the engagement took place.

And Sisi, the child-bride of fifteen and three-quarters, what were her feelings? Well, "her heart was yet unawakened; but love had found its way into her dreams" (C. Tschudi); and when asked whether she returned Franz Josef's love she is said to have replied, "Yes, yes, if only he weren't an Emperor!" Later, she became rather more specific about her idea of her husband's occupation, "If only he were a tailor!"

This would in fact have been far better for all concerned. – Or if Ludovika had left her Elisabeth at home the Emperor would have taken Nené, and he would have been spared much. Even a "No" from Sisi is imaginable as a good alternative – although it would probably not have been much use; her mother and mother-in-law had not married their husbands for pleasure either – the faithless Max and the friendly, but rather simple Archduke Franz Carl. Princely marriages were contracted for reasons of state, not out of personal inclination. In the rare cases when both coincided, this was considered all the more pleasing.

The Emperor's mother, Sophie, was admittedly unenthusiastic about her son's choice but did not care to continue to push for Helene; Ludovika and Duke Max were satisfied. The Austrian people likewise. They made a poem out of it and sang:

„Rose aus Bayerland,
Lieblich und traut,
Nun grüßt Dich ganz Öst'reich
Als hehre Braut!"

("Rose from Bavaria,
Lovely and dear,
Now all Austria greets you,
As the exalted bride!")

A Sisi monument in the grounds of Hellbrunn Castle near Salzburg. The statue is made of marble in a white to grey-green-black colour. Just why it was placed here is explained in the inscription on the base: "Your Austria, You represented her here / As the Emperor's bride in sweet majesty, / All hearts you did win / Your joyous greeting was a blessing, was a prayer."

Lith. v. A. Ziegler.   Gedr. b. J. Höfelich's Wwe in Wien.   Joh. Schnickl's Fest-Woche

Sisi Weeps

Nine months elapsed between the engagement at Bad Ischl and the wedding in Vienna; nine months for the – not exactly cultivated – Imperial bride to be prepared for her high dignity. Austrian history, French, Italian, dancing, court protocol and small-talk were on the curriculum.

On 20th April 1854 she left Munich. The people came in droves. "Overcome by the pangs of departure, she rose in her carriage and with tear-filled eyes waved her farewell to the crowd that bade her good-bye." – The coach travelled to Straubing. There Sisi was greeted with cheering and congratulations; speeches were given, flags waved, music played. Sisi cried, Sisi waved. The next morning she – together with her mother, father, brother Ludwig and sister Nené – boarded the Danube steamer "City of Regensburg."

On the 21st, at around two in the afternoon, the wedding party arrived at Passau on the border with Austria. An Imperial deputation appeared on board, and greeted the bride; at six in the afternoon the boat arrived in Linz. Schoolchildren and

Accompanied by her parents and by her brother Ludwig and sister Helene, the young bride leaves Munich on 20 April 1854. Behind the dapple-grey horses is the Siegestor (Victory Arch) in Munich, and lining the streets waving their farewell are the loyal people of Bavaria.

The Danube at Nussdorf, the final stop on Sisi's journey aboard a Danube steamer. Sisi arrived here on 22 April at four in the afternoon, to the joyous welcome of the citizens and officials of the town. She then travelled further across land to Schönbrunn. In the background are the Kahlenberg and Leopoldsberg mountains.

soldiers, nobles, clergy and citizens were all afoot to receive the future Empress with flowers, torchlight processions, bonfires, choral singing, civic illuminations and theatrical performances. The Emperor – to surprise her, he had set off by steamboat from Vienna in the small hours – was already waiting. Sisi cried, Sisi waved. Brutal – modern – Sisi-critics scold the poor child, "Nevertheless, there was fundamentally nothing about the situation to justify such a distressed response. An emotionally healthy girl of that age would surely have presented herself quite differently, profiting from the positive aspects of the spectacle and the affection that lay behind it." Sisi's behaviour is viewed as "the first noticeable psychiatric disturbance, in the form of recurring moods of anxiety and depression." (F. E. Schilke)

The day after, at eight in the morning, the voyage continued on the paddle steamer "Franz Josef," splendidly decked with roses. Work stopped on this joyful day, the people of Austria had leisure to rejoice, wave flags, ring bells and fire guns in salute. "On board ship," we learn from

On the afternoon of 23 April the traditional festival procession of the Emperor's bride into the city of Vienna took place with great pomp and ceremony. The route led from the Theresianum to the Hofburg. Vienna rejoiced, Sisi cried bitterly.

Franz Josef and Sisi walking on Gloriette Hill, from where they have an excellent view of the grounds of Schönbrunn Castle and the city of Vienna. "All this" he said to his young bride, "belongs to me." Or something similar.

Clara Tschudi "a figure in a light-coloured dress could be seen running from one side to the other. Although constantly required to return thanks for the tumultuous greetings she did not appear to tire." The strains of the Imperial hymn were heard everywhere, and after the wedding it was lengthened by the Biedermeier lyricist and teacher Johann Gabriel Seidl, to bring it up to date:

„An des Kaisers Seite waltet, / Ihm verwandt durch Stamm und Sinn, / Reich an Reiz, der nie veraltet, / Unsere holde Kaiserin. / Was das Glück zu höchst gepriesen, / Ström' auf sie der Himmel aus! / Heil Franz Joseph, Heil Elisen, / Segen Habsburgs ganzem Haus."

("At the Emperor's side holds sway, / Akin to him in lineage and mind, / Rich in charm which never ages, / Our Imperial Empress. / Let the fortune which has exalted her to the highest / Stream down on her from Heaven! / Hail Franz Josef, hail Elisa, / Blessings on the whole House of Hapsburg.")

Around four in the afternoon the "Franz Josef" was calling in at Nussdorf, or had only just berthed, when the Emperor sprang aboard the ship, took his bride in his arms and kissed her heartily – a proceeding that aroused much joyous interest and emotion.

Then the Hapsburg relations were presented to her, the bells rang out, the Cardinal Archbishop spoke, music played, cannons thundered, flowers were strewn, and then they continued, now by coach, to Schönbrunn, the Imperial summer residence; at the head the Emperor with Max, the father of the bride, behind Sisi with her mother-in-law, after her Ludovika with the Emperor's father, finally the rest of the families.

Triumphal arches had been erected, the crowd roared their hurrahs and loyal sentiments, and at half-past six they arrived

at Schönbrunn; Sisi, tired, pale and embarrassed, waved and wept.

23rd April: the traditional ceremonial entrance of the Imperial bride into the city of Vienna. Stands had been erected for the public, guns fired, bells rang. "In the Kärntnerstrasse almost every house shimmered in a true glory of lamps, candles and gaslights amongst draperies, allegories, flags, coats of arms, flowers, in short all imaginable opulence." (F. B. Tschudy). Sisi sat weeping with her mother in the state coach drawn by eight Lippizaner steeds, the court carriages, court trumpeters and bodyguards accompanying her. Sisi waved.

24th April, seven in the evening: the wedding ceremony in the Augustinerkirche. 15,000 candles burned, a thousand invited guests were present. "The bright uniforms of the officers, the colourful and picturesque ceremonial dress of the Hungarian and Polish nobility, the glittering jewels of the ladies, the gold-embroidered garments of the ministers and high officials, the cardinals' red cassocks, the fantastic garb of several of the oriental envoys – all combined to make a picture fit for a fairy-tale" (C. Tschudi).

The Archbishop of Vienna conducted the wedding and gave an almost never-ending speech; Sisi's love was "to be like an island for the Emperor in the midst of his cares of state, lying verdant and peace-

Previous double page:

Here again we see the Baroque Imperial Summer Residence of Schönbrunn, this time in a water colour by Robert Raschka. 2.7 million visitors come here each year. The castle has 1441 rooms, but visitors are only allowed to see about 45 of them, but that is quite enough anyway. Franz Josef was born in this castle in 1830, and this is where he died.

The whole of Vienna was on its feet when the Imperial couple celebrated their wedding. The city, here at the Platz an der Freyung – was gloriously illuminated.

On 24 April 1854 at 7 in the evening Franz Josef and Sisi were married in the Augustiner Church, by Archbishop Cardinal Rauscher. In view of the fact that they were close relations (their mothers were sisters), they needed a special dispensation from the Pope.

ful among the stormy waves, bringing forth the smiling rose and the charming violet" – a kind wish, unfortunately only imperfectly fulfilled.

On the return in ceremonial procession to the Hofburg, the Imperial palace, there followed an extensive programme of courtly congratulations and audiences.

The new Empress was introduced to generals, ambassadors, envoys and their wives and the entire royal household, who did not interest her in the least. Sisi was completely exhausted. And she cried.

The demand for pictures of the rulers is always very high in monarchist countries. And so business was good for the portraitists. And whenever a jubilee or marriage takes place, the painters and drawers are especially busy.

Early Regrets of an Early Marriage

Now Sisi was the Empress of the second largest state in Europe (after Russia). At the age of sixteen and a quarter.

She spent the honeymoon in the Imperial pleasure palace of Laxenburg. Her Bavarian staff had been sent home and replaced with hand-picked Court employees loyal to her mother-in-law. The Emperor went to work every morning; he needed to reign in the Hofburg, and did not come home until dinner-time at six.

On the other hand his mother, Sophie, that "spiteful woman," was all the more in evidence.

Sophie had turned her son into an Emperor; now the shy, insecure, unpolished Bavarian country child was to become a worthy Hapsburg Empress. Sophie disciplined, admonished and instructed her daughter-in-law, put her in leading-reins, squashed her, "trampled arrogantly over all her hopes and dispelled her dreams and longings with a heavy hand," writes Clara Tschudi. – This was not done, that was forbidden; an Imperial couple might not attend the theatre unescorted, an Em-

Sophie, mother of the Emperor and aunt to Sisi. She was the real ruler, it was she ensured that in 1848, after the abdication of Emperor Ferdinand I, who was mentally ill, her naive husband, Archduke Franz Carl waived his claim to the Imperial throne in favour of her devoted son, Franz Josef. Her daughter-in-law hated her.

There are not only four dozen rooms to see in Schönbrunn – also well worth seeing is the Baroque, French-style Castle Park, and the Wagenburg, in which the best item displayed is the gilded Imperial coach.

press could not go riding alone or follow her husband to Vienna; she must be elegantly dressed at all times and wear gloves continually. Forced into court ceremonial, steered and controlled by protocol, spied upon and watched by the intimates of the Emperor's mother, treated as a child under age (which she in fact was), rejected by the royal household for being too provincial and for lacking refinement, wealth or elegance, Sisi languished at the Viennese court in a chronically offended condition. She played with her dogs, talked to her parrots, rode, and coughed; she loathed her mother-in-law, detested her imprisonment, the ladies in waiting, the court balls, the receptions, and the restrictions on dress; vacillating

between attempts to adapt and rebellion, she was homesick for her idyllic Possenhofen with its natural, cordial atmosphere, and for the informality of Munich.

She wrote in her poetry notebook:

Doch was ist mir die Frühlingswonne,
Hier in dem fernen, fremden Land?
Ich sehn' mich nach der Heimat Sonne.
Ich sehn' mich nach der Isar Strand.

(But what are the delights of spring to me,
Here in this distant, alien land?
I yearn for the sun of my homeland,
I yearn for the banks of the Isar.)

From her husband, whom she indeed dearly loved but who had no emotional intuition, she had little support. He refused to be involved; he had always been accustomed to obeying his mother.

Neither was the young Empress much delighted with married life. She was fond of her Franz Josef but the proceedings in the Imperial bed bewildered her and, according to Clara Tschudi, "she was always somewhat shy of passionate feelings and preserved in her relations with him the purity of a childlike soul."

She mourned her lost childhood. A fortnight after the wedding she wrote, full of regret, both a little early and too late:

Oh, daß ich nie den Pfad verlassen,
Der mich zur Freiheit hätt' geführt.
Oh, daß ich auf der breiten Straßen
Der Eitelkeit mich nie verirrt!

Ich bin erwacht in einem Kerker,
Und Fesseln sind an meiner Hand,
Und meine Sehnsucht immer stärker –
Und Freiheit! Du mir abgewandt!

Ich bin erwacht aus einem Rausche,
Der meinen Geist gefangenhielt,
Und fluche fruchtlos diesem Tausche,
Bei dem ich Freiheit! Dich verspielt.

(O, that I had never left that path
Which would have led me to freedom.
O, that I had never strayed down the broad
highways of vanity!

I have awakened in a prison cell
And fetters are upon my wrist,
And my yearning grows ever stronger –
And freedom! thou hast turned thy face from me!

I have awakened from a delusion
Which held my spirit prisoner,
And try vainly to escape what I exchanged
For thee, O freedom! whom I gambled away!)

She was, sobs Clara Tschudi, "a true-

A beautiful Sisi monument stands in the Volksgarten in Vienna, another in Feldafing in the park of the "Golf Hotel Empress Elisabeth," a third (see p. 29) in Hellbrunn. And yet another is under cover, in the rooms open to public view in the Hofburg.

A Hapsburg family portrait. From left to right we see: the Emperor's mother, Sophie, with her granddaughter Gisela on her lap, her husband, Franz Carl, Elisabeth, Franz Josef and between his father's knees, his eldest daughter Sophie (born 1855, died 1858).

hearted, naive nature, a poor little bird who has abandoned the family nest before it has learned to fly."

Soon she became pregnant. In March 1855 her first daughter, Sophie, came into the world (and died two years later, on a trip to Hungary), in July 1856 Gisela was born, and in 1858 the necessary Crown Prince, Rudolf. So Sisi had done her duty.

She rebelled against her mother-in-law, who also took over her grandchildren's upbringing, snubbed Court society, and occupied herself with starvation diets – to restore her slender, pre-motherhood figure – grew exhausted after three confinements in four years, and became irritable and nervous. And sickly and tearful.

In June 1859 the Emperor went to war,

fighting against France and Italy, and took the military command into his own inexpert hands, without success. Sisi, now quite alone, without friends in Vienna, harrassed by a phalanx of disapproving female opponents, remained at home, the soldier's wife; wanting to go to her husband but not permitted to, she sought distraction in equestrianism; obstinately and intractably opposed to Sophie, she wept.

Far Away From Vienna

In the summer of 1859 Franz Josef returned from Italy. Circumstances at Court had shown no signs of improvement; family divisions and wrangling simmered on, putting the Emperor more and more out of temper. He consoled himself with an unnamed Polish countess and other friendly ladies. Sisi heard of it, was appalled and deeply insulted. "The Emperor, who feared a scandal, confessed his misdeeds, fell at Elisabeth's feet; in great distress he begged her forgiveness and promised, like a child, never to do it again" (H. de Weindel): but nothing he could do was now any good; Sisi fell ill.

What was wrong with her tradition does not make clear. Swellings in wrists and knees were noted; a rash on her face, a cough and a sore throat. Officially, she had a disease of the lungs; unofficially, the word went round that she had venereal disease, and that the Emperor had infected his wife. A third interpretation is that the illness was only a pretext, because the people could not very well be told, "Elisabeth has had enough of Vienna and her Empress's throne, of her husband and her mother-in-law. Her love is over; as a mother she is not required, and she refuses to act as a decorative figurine."

After six years of marriage Sisi, now 22,

left the Imperial house and court and travelled to Madeira. – Why Madeira? Was there no nearer destination, even better for the lungs, perhaps, such as Merano or Abbazia? There were indeed, but Elisabeth wanted to be as far away as possible from the court she detested, and from the unfaithful Emperor.

On 17th November 1860 she set out. She left her children, Gisela, four, and Rudolf, two, behind. The world was full of sympathy; the Queen of England put a yacht at her disposal. The crossing from Antwerp to Madeira was stormy, but Sisi rode out the waves with good appetite, and to the amazement of the islanders, who had expected a wasted and mortally ill patient, she arrived at Funchal three-quarters recovered. She took a villa at the outskirts of the capital with a view over the Atlantic, a terrace, and a garden; she enjoyed the splendours of nature, revelled in the vernal climate and the display of blossom, bought ponies and a large dog, rambled, flirted with her equerries, and permitted herself to be admired, acquiring, now that she was free from the court, a proud self-assurance. Towards Christmas she began to grow bored; she read Shakespeare, she read the poems of Heinrich Heine, played old maid, plucked at the mandolin, and left the island on 28th April 1861.

"Her heart." we learn from Faye's biography, "demanded the sweet caresses of her children, her eyes desired to see no other horizons than the innocent clarity of their eyes. Feverishly she counted the hours – the minutes – that separated her from her loved ones." – Counting the minutes, however, did not stop her taking her time over her homeward journey. She visited Cadiz and Seville, Gibraltar, Majorca, Malta, Corfu, met the Emperor in Trieste and travelled with him to Vienna, blooming, healthy and beautiful. Her children no longer knew her.

Madeira's soft, gentle climate, with an average of 16 °C in winter and 21 °C in summer, makes this island particularly popular with older or convalescent people. Tropical vegetation grows readily in parks and hotel gardens.

Following double page:

Corfu, the northernmost of the Ionian islands, has pleasant, sandy beaches and a warm blue sea; it has limestone mountains in the north and lush green hills in the south. The Empress fled to Corfu in the summer of 1861. Later she built her house, Achilleion, here.

Hardly had she reached Vienna, received with overwhelming enthusiasm by the populace, than war with the Archduchess broke out once more. Sisi stormed off to Laxenburg Palace, and refused to appear at any court dinners or receptions. A past mistress at sudden illnesses and recoveries, she immediately began to cough again, suffering as usual from weakness, anaemia, exhaustion, sore throats, fever, insomnia and loss of appetite.

The doctors diagnosed galloping consumption and declared, "Six more weeks in Vienna will be the death of her." She had to hasten to the south, and set off on 23rd June, this time for Corfu, where she arrived on the 27th – by now almost cured. She lived in the Governor's coun-

try residence, went on long walks, sailed, bathed in the sea, against all medical advice, and went on starvation diets to make her slim.

Sister Helene came to visit, the Emperor sent couriers. The news which reached him from Corfu was contradictory: Sisi was suntanned, she was deathly pale; cheerful but melancholy; cheerful, lovelier than ever, but her face was swollen. On 13th October the Emperor himself appeared on the island, and Elisabeth decided that she would quite definitely not spend the winter in Vienna but in Venice instead, which was nevertheless still – in those days – on Hapsburg soil. The children would have to come there, if only to upset her mother-in-law. Sisi read much

and went sailing, but her stay did not revive her and the Venetian nobility was stand-offish. Soon Sisi's feet swelled again, her face looked puffy, and she was plagued by anaemia and hunger oedema. She stayed in Venice for seven months, till the end of May, and finally underwent an oedema cure in Kissingen, spent a few weeks with her Bavarian family and arrived in Vienna on 14th August, in time for the Emperor's birthday; she had been absent almost two years and had grown more mature and even lovelier, full of energy and self-confidence. She said to the happy Viennese: "I will hope that the pleasure of being amongst you once more will continue and that nothing will cloud it." – The Emperor treated her with circumspection and indulgent patience; he knew that the slightest provocation would be enough to cloud her happiness and make her vanish once again.

Empress of Beauty

Sisi had "not one single pretty feature," her mother lamented to Marie of Saxony in the April of 1853. This is by far and wide the only negative view of Sisi's beauty. Otherwise all her contemporaries and biographers are united: Sisi was almost incredibly charming and attractive; even her mother-in-law, whom one could hardly suspect of extravagant praise, found her "as lovely as an angel."

Clara Tschudi described Elisabeth as a bride: "Her form was tall and extraordinarily slender, her hands and feet small and well-shaped. Her childlike features were regular and fine. Around her lips there sometimes played a delightful smile, readily displayed in earlier, happier days. Her eyes were dark blue and full of

depth. Her skin was like milk and blood, and gave an impression of remarkable beauty when framed by her dark hair, which fell around her like a long thick cloak when she loosened it. Sometimes she would let it fall in eight heavy braids around her shoulders, sometimes she wound it like a diadem about her head." – Nevertheless, attentive observers could even then discern that her eyes held "thoughts of illimitable depths, tokens of the mysteries of her soul, which she was soon to present as an insoluble enigma to the curious world." (F. Gribble).

The German Kaiser Wilhelm II is said to have described her "all his life as the most beautiful woman in the world"; his General Moltke in 1865 found Elisabeth "even more attractive than beautiful", and the Prussian Crown Princess Victoria wrote in 1862, "Her admittedly not quite regular beauty is unsurpassable. I have never seen anything quite so dazzling or so piquant. Her features are not as lovely

Romy Schneider as Sisi with diamonds and stars in her plaited hair. The star-in-the-hair motif is a must for every actress playing Empress Elisabeth.

The idea for the diamond hair ornament came from a painting by Franz Xaver Winterhalter, the most famous of all Sisi portraits; it showed her in 1864, wearing a ball gown.

as most of the pictures show them, but the general impression is more charming than any painting in the world could even remotely reproduce."

"In the 1860s and 1870s Elisabeth was regarded as the most beautiful woman in the world. People travelled to Vienna to admire her, she was a tourist attraction", we learn from a Hungarian catalogue of a Sisi exhibition, and also, "that when the Empress appeared a sigh could clearly be heard from the lips of those present; not for the Empress but, above all, for the most beautiful woman in the world."

The American envoy to Vienna called her "a miracle of beauty – tall and slender, with a wonderfully lovely figure, an abundance of light brown hair, a low Grecian forehead, soft eyes, very red lips and a sweet smile", and even Nasr-ed-Din, the vicious Shah of Persia, fell speechless when he saw her at the International Exhibition in Vienna in 1873. He is even said to have considered buying her from the Austrian Emperor – which would not have been such a bad solution – but the deal never came off.

Maria Wallersee recalled her first encounter with the Empress: "Elisabeth seemed to me a daughter of sun and fire as she sat there in the golden morning, which heightened still further the loveliness and strangeness of her unearthly presence". Her colleague Marie Festetics noted in her diary in 1872: "She is the embodiment of the word loveliness. One moment I think her a lily, the next a swan, a fairy or an elf. Wrong again – a queen! A royal lady from top to toe! Refined and noble in all things."

How is such wondrous beauty achieved, and, next, how is it kept? Baroness Wallersee betrays some recipes for cosmetics to us. At night she wore "a sort of mask, lined inside with raw veal" or she smeared her hands and neck with crushed strawberries. She kept her skin supple with baths of warm olive oil, and she slept "in a simple iron bedstead, which she carried with her on all her journeyings. She scorned pillows and lay quite flat, probably because someone had once persuaded her that this would benefit her beauty." She was also "in the habit of drinking a dreadful mixture of five or six raw eggs and salt," to keep her young and beautiful. Otherwise, so our informant Francis Gribble tells us, she used distilled water for bathing.

Her hair, when loose reaching to her knees or her ankles, was her greatest pride. Every three weeks it was washed with raw eggs and brandy, a procedure which took an entire day, including drying. "After washing her hair, the Empress would don a long, waterproof silk dressing gown and walk up and down until her hair dried." (M. Wallersee) Without washing and setting it took three hours each day to dress her hair.

Sisi's beauty had just one flaw; her carious yellowish-brown teeth. Although she had come into the world with two

This is Nasr-ed-Din, the wild Shah of Persia, born in 1829 and on the peacock throne since 1848. In 1873 he came to the World Exhibition in Vienna, and was lodged in Laxenburg Castle, where he caused a stir by slaughtering chickens and sheep himself.

The third Winterhalter picture of Sisi (here a copy by Riegele): the Empress with her hair falling down over her shoulders to her knees; some sources even say it reached to her ankles.

Franz Schrotzberg's picture of Sisi is one of the few for which the Empress actually posed as model. She only conferred this honour on Piloty and Winterhalter. The other painters had to content themselves with fleeting glimpses or photographs.

teeth – from the purely dental point of view a good omen – her teeth were in a bad state. Even at Ischl the Archduchess Sophie had disapproved of them at some length. When it became clear that not even brushing was much use Elisabeth decided she would simply hide her teeth by pulling her upper lip down over them, barely opening her mouth, and holding a handkerchief in front of it – which rather impeded conversation with her. "Those who did not know Elisabeth well," reports Maria Wallersee," had the utmost difficulty in understanding her. "It was

Sisi, as slender as a reed and light as a feather. To achieve her 50-cm waistline she starved herself half to death and laced herself in until she could hardly breathe. The painting is by Franz Russ.

not until she was well advanced in years that she wore false teeth. Her deft handling of them is described by the actress Rosa Albach-Retty, who once observed her in a country inn in Ischl: "Elisabeth glanced in front of her for a second, reached for her false teeth with her left hand, took them out, held them sideways over the edge of the table and rinsed them in a glass of water. Then she slipped them back in her mouth. This was all done with so much gracious nonchalance, above all with such lightning speed, that at first I could not believe my eyes."

Sisi was 1 metre 72 tall. Her waist measured 50 centimetres (the lady guide at the Imperial villa in Bad Ischl actually asserts; only 40) and throughout her life she took great pains to stop her weight exceeding 50 kilograms. (Today the approved normal weight for a woman of her height is a good 60 kilograms).

Elisabeth's Greek tutor, Constantin Christomanos, expressed his enthusiasm as late as 1891, when she was in fact 54 years old: "Her whole form, too flowing to be termed merely slender, sighs heavenwards like a cypress, flows like a wave when she rests and draws breath." – Mother Ludovika however thought she was as "thin as a beanpole."

She maintained this thinness by frequently wrapping herself in damp cloths above the hips and by rigorous self-prescribed and highly effective slimming regimes and starvation diets, which she at times also imposed on her entourage.

"She eats frightfully little," complained Count Rechberg, whom the Emperor had sent to Madeira, "and the result is that we must all suffer from it, because the meal, four dishes, four desserts, coffee, etc. never lasts longer than twenty-five minutes." Indeed it was not – and probably still is not – permitted at Court for anyone to continue eating once the Royal

Presence had laid down his or her spoon.

From time to time she would partake only of pressed extract of raw chicken, partridge, venison and beef ; for weeks on end she would eat nothing but eggs, oranges and raw milk.

A photograph of Sisi from 1865, by her personal photographer, Victor Angerer. Up until about 1870 she enjoyed having her photograph taken. But not after that.

Sisi's bathroom in the Hof-burg in Vienna. Here she began every day with a cold bath at about five or six in the morning. She also favoured baths of warm olive oil, to keep her skin soft. However, we can imagine that she didn't smell very nice after such a bath.

Milk was her favourite drink, fresh from the cow but not just any cow. There are cows and there are cows; one may yield excellent milk, another milk with a far inferior flavour; the modern consumer of ultra-heat treated, pasteurised, homo-genised, ultra-purified , skimmed long-life milk in tetra-bricks no longer has any notion of it. Sisi therefore liked to take her own tried and tested cows from the Vienna dairy farm on her travels with her. If she met a particularly fine dairy cow en

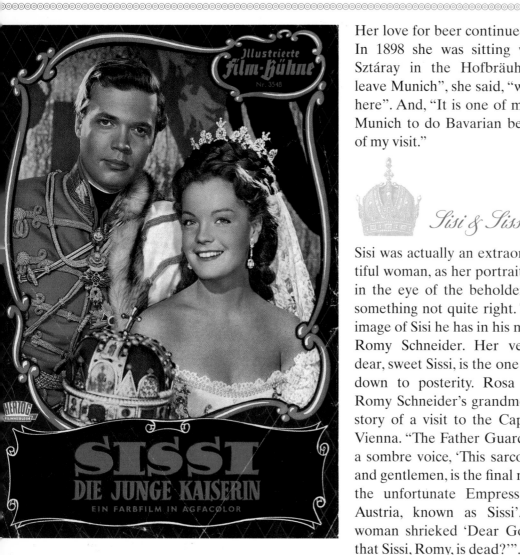

Her love for beer continued to her death. In 1898 she was sitting with Countess Sztáray in the Hofbräuhaus. "I never leave Munich", she said, "without coming here". And, "It is one of my traditions in Munich to do Bavarian beer the honour of my visit."

Sisi & Sissi

Sisi was actually an extraordinarily beautiful woman, as her portraits confirm. But in the eye of the beholder, there is still something not quite right. This is not the image of Sisi he has in his mind, this is not Romy Schneider. Her version of Sisi, dear, sweet Sissi, is the one that is handed down to posterity. Rosa Albach-Retty, Romy Schneider's grandmother, tells the story of a visit to the Capucin Crypt in Vienna. "The Father Guardian told us, in a sombre voice, 'This sarcophagus, ladies and gentlemen, is the final resting place of the unfortunate Empress Elisabeth of Austria, known as Sissi'. Horrified, a woman shrieked 'Dear God! You mean that Sissi, Romy, is dead?'".

The three famous Ernst Marischka Sissi films from the time of Soraya and Gracia Patricia, in 1955, 56 and 57, were preceded by a "Princess Sissy" film made in 1938.

In this film Sissy is still a child, living a happy, carefree existence in Possenhofen. A blaze puts paid to a travelling circus and Sissy's father, Max, saves it from bankruptcy by putting on a dressage and trick riding act with his friends and Sissy. As such extravaganzas are a thoroughly improper way for a duke to behave, King Ludwig I becomes angry and wants to have these noble acrobats arrested. However, little Sissy is able to pacify him and all ends happily. The cranky old duke was

route it was bought and sent to Schönbrunn.

She enjoyed icecream, and also oysters. What though – an interesting side-light – did this Wittelsbach from Bavaria think of beer?

"This brown liquid", she told the Countess Sztáray, "is not my favourite drink." Nevertheless she did full justice to it and as a brand-new Empress at the Viennese court she unleashed a "storm of outrage" when she demanded – for breakfast, too, – "bread, sausage and a glass of Munich beer" (which, of course, she didn't get). – In 1861 a relieved Princess Helene told her mother from Corfu that Sisi "is drinking a lot of beer".

In 1956 Ernst Marischka made the colour film "Sissi, the young Empress". The success of the Sissi films was enormous; the 1950s audience were very taken by the events in the nobility and at court. Karlheinz Böhm played the young Emperor and Romy Schneider his Empress. It took Ms Schneider a long time to cast off this image.

The film Sissi, recently married. Field Marshall Radetzky (Otto Tressler) congratulates her. Behind him is Nené (Uta Franz). Beside Emperor Karlheinz Böhm is Peter Weck as a moody Archduke Carl Ludwig, for he was secretly in love with the beautiful Elisabeth.

played by Paul Hörbiger, his wife Ludovika by Gerda Maurus and Sissy by Traudl Stark (Director: Fritz Thiery).

The most touching point of Sisi's biography was the engagement at Ischl. In 1932, Ernst and Hubert Marischka (with music by Fritz Kreisler) staged the lyrical drama "Sissy". Ludovika and her daughter Nené, who was to be betrothed to Franz Josef, are travelling to Ischl. In their excitement, the two of them leave Nené's silver court dress at home. Father Max and Sissy follow them, uninvited. Sissy, the boxed dress under her arm, picks roses in the garden of the Imperial villa and Franz Josef, watching her, thinks she is a seamstress and falls in love with her. After a number of intrigues, he discovers who Sissy really is and becomes engaged to her. Nené, however, who did not really want the Emperor, snares the Prince von Thurn und Taxis, whom she loves. The operetta did not become particularly famous, especially as it lacked any really

catchy tunes. Nevertheless, it is still performed every now and then at Bad Ischl.

In 1954, Helmut Käutner filmed "Ludwig II. The Glory and Death of a King", with Ruth Leuwerik as Sisi and O. W. Fischer as Ludwig II.

Ernst Marischka's first "Sissi" film appeared one year later. Once again, Ischl was the starting point. Franz Josef and Sissi meet by chance, as Sissi is going fishing and by the evening, at dinner in the Imperial villa, they are already celebrating their betrothal. Sissi journeys to a rejoicing Vienna on a ship bedecked with roses. The film ends with the wedding. This is the first time that Romy Schneider portrayed Sissi. Karlheinz Böhm played the young Emperor, Magda Schneider was Sissi's mother Ludovika and Gustav Knuth was Duke Maximilian.

The sequel followed in 1956: "Sissi, the Young Empress". Sophie, the first of the Emperor's daughters, is born. Everyone loves Sissi, apart from her wicked,

scheming mother-in-law. Filled with despair, Sissi flees to Possenhofen. Franz Josef, however, lovingly fetches her back, journeys with her up into the mountains and from Heiligenblut, climbs half-way up the Grossglockner (his monument is still there today, on the Franz-Josefs-Höhe). Sissi brings about reconciliation with Hungary and King and Queen are crowned in Budapest.

In 1957, the public enjoyed "Empress Sissi – the Fateful Years". Sissi, still portrayed by Romy Schneider, is staying with her daughter Sophie in Hungary and wicked enemies accuse her of having an affair with Count Andrássy. She takes a holiday in Ischl, contracts tuberculosis, but is cured in Madeira and Corfu. She and the Emperor travel to Italy, where the aristocracy disapprove of her. The people, however, instantly fall under the spell of the beautiful Empress and there is a happy ending in St. Mark's Square, in Venice.

Empress & King

Empress Elisabeth of Austria and King Ludwig of Bavaria, the two are cousins – she, the "most beautiful woman in the world", and the quaintly romantic monarch, "bathed in all the charm of youthful beauty", what a pair!

In June 1864, she 26, he 18, they got to know each other better in Kissingen. They went on long walks together, held deep, meaningful conversations and came to realise how much their souls were in harmony.

Their friendship was long-lasting. They met when the Empress was staying at Lake Starnberg, on the nearby Rose Island and in Possenhofen Castle. He gave her flowers, kissed her hand, they wrote to each other and penned sincere poems.

Sisi had a very close and dear friendship with her cousin, the beautiful King Ludwig II of Bavaria. Both were dreamers and illusionists, shy of people and above the banal world and its doings. Sometimes, however, they disagreed, as, for example, in 1867 when he rather abruptly ended his engagement to Sisi's sister, Sophie.

Du Adler, dort hoch auf den Bergen, / Dir schickt die Möve der See / Einen Gruss von schäumenden Wogen / Hinauf zum ewigen Schnee.
Einst sind wir einander begegnet / Vor urgrauer Ewigkeit / Am Spiegel des lieblichsten Sees, / Zur blühenden Rosenzeit.

(Oh eagle, high on the mountains, / The gull from the sea sends you / Greetings from the foaming waves / To the heights, to the eternal snow.
We met once upon a time / A dim and distant eternity ago / At water level, on the most delightful lake / When the roses were in full bloom.)

went her rhyme (1885) and Ludwig responded with the following verse:

„*Der Möve Gruss von fernem Strand / Zu Adlers Horst den Weg wohl fand. / Er trug auf leisem Fittig-Schwung / Der alten Zeit Erinnerung.*"

("From far-flung shores the seagull's greeting / To the eagle's nest its way did find. / Bearing with it on soft flitting wing / Sweet memories of old times.")

He admired her, calling himself her "de- voted slave, who will adore you for always and for ever". When, in July 1867, he had accompanied the Empress to Austria on the train, he wrote to her. "My dear cous- in, you can have no idea how happy that made me. I count the hours recently spent in the railway carriage as some of the happiest of my life. The memory will nev- er fade."

Eroticism, despite unqualified state- ments to the contrary made by impudent moralists, played no part in the relation- ship. The "chaste King" indignantly rejected that kind of thing, especially with women. "In most young people," he once wrote, "sensuality interferes with their affection for the opposite sex; I heartily condemn this." In any case, Elisa- beth was not well disposed towards sen- sual love:

Lang geh ich schon hinieden um,
Mich macht die Liebe schauern

In 1864 in Kissingen Ludwig and Elisabeth got to know each other better. The lady on the right of the picture in the billowing dress is Sisi, and behind her to one side, her father, Max. The tall man in the round hat is the Russian Tsar, Alexander II. To the left, in the top hat, is the Bavarian King, Ludwig, and beside him Tsarina Marie.

On the secluded "Roseninsel" island in Feldafing Bay on Lake Starnberg Sisi and Ludwig used to meet. Surrounded by the sweet scent of roses, they exchanged their muddled thoughts. The distance Sisi sits from the King may have something to do with the perfume he used to use rather lavishly. Sisi hated the smell of perfume.

(Long have I been on this earth,
For love makes me shudder)

she wrote and mentioned as laudable her friendship with Count Andrássy, which was "not poisoned by love".

Ludwig and Elisabeth suited each other to an almost frightening degree. They were both eccentric, egocentric, unsociable, melancholic and extravagant; they shared the elitist feeling that nobody understood them; they both ran away from their duties and wrapped themselves up in their sickness and suffering in the same way; they even had the same bad teeth. Sisi hated Vienna, Ludwig Munich; she felt locked up in her "prison cell of a castle", he in his "golden cage".

From time to time, however, the peaceful harmony was disturbed. Sometimes the infatuated king got on her nerves and she complained "If only the King of Bavaria would leave me in peace!" For his part, he found the detailed stories about her favourite daughter, Valerie, rather boring. In 1867, when Ludwig became betrothed to Sisi's sister Sophie, but then instantly regretted it, and put off the wed-

ding several times before finally breaking the engagement, she was furious with him. "You can imagine just how infuriated I am about the King, the Emperor is as well," she wrote to her mother, but added by way of consolation, "God knows she could never have been happy with such a man!"

When, in 1886, the King was declared to be mentally ill, was deposed and interned in Berg Castle, finally to drown in Lake Starnberg, Sisi was living in Feldafing. There were rumours that she had sent a coach for him, to help him escape. However, there is absolutely no evidence to support this.

Nevertheless, shortly after his death, the King appeared to her in person. Sisi's niece, the Baroness Wallersee, wrote down what the Empress told her:

"The moon had risen and the moonlight made the room as bright as day. I watched as the door slowly opened and Ludwig came in.

His clothes were heavy with water, which dripped off him and formed little pools on the parquet floor. His wet hair

was plastered round his white face, but it was clearly Ludwig, just as he had looked when he was alive.

We stared at one another in silence and then the King said, slowly and sadly,

'Are you afraid of me, Sisi?'

'No Ludwig, I'm not afraid.'

'Oh dear', he sighed, 'death has brought me no rest, Sissi. She is burning to death in agony. The flames flicker round her, she chokes on the smoke. She is burning to death and I cannot save her.'

'Who is burning to death, dear cousin?' I asked.

'I do not know, for her face is hidden,' he replied, 'but I do know that it is a woman who has loved me and until her fate is decided, I will not be free. But afterwards, you will encounter us and we

three will be happy together in paradise.'

'What does this mean? When am I to meet you?'

'I cannot say,' replied Ludwig, 'for in the kingdom of souls, there is no such thing as time.'

'On which road am I to meet you? Will it be a journey through a painful old age full of remorse and remembrance?'

'No, Sissi,' said my cousin, 'you may well shed many tears and become acquainted with remorse and remembrance, before you come to us. But your journey will reach a rapid, sudden end.'

'Will I have to suffer?'

He smiled. 'No, you will not suffer.'

'How am I to know that I am not dreaming?' I asked.

Ludwig slowly approached my bed, the

In summer Ludwig liked to stay in Berg Castle on the east bank of Lake Starnberg. The building dates from the 17th century, and Ludwig's father had it embellished with Gothicist corner turrets and battlements; these additions were removed in 1949. A small chapel in the castle park stands in memorial of the King who drowned here in the lake in 1886.

coldness of death and of the grave gave a chill to the air. 'Give me your hand,' he commanded.

I stretched out my hand and his wet fingers enclosed them. At that moment, compassion welled up in me. 'Please stay', I cried, 'do not leave your friend, who loves you, to return to your suffering. Oh Ludwig, pray with me that you shall have your peace.'

But while I was speaking, the figure disappeared."

Elisabeth assured her niece that the story was "true, every word of it" and that it certainly had not been a dream. The Empress later recognised the burning lady as being her sister Sophie, Ludwig's former betrothed, who died a terrible death in a fire at a charity event in Paris in 1897.

Sisi and the Magyars

Sisi showed no more enthusiasm for politics than she showed for most other things connected with her duties as Empress. "I also have too little respect for politics and consider it not worthy of my interest," she confided to her Greek tutor, Christomanos. His successor, Marinaky, quoted her as saying, "However, I detest modern politics and consider it to be full of lies and deceit."

The uprisings of 1848/49 in Northern Italy and Hungary had been before her time. In the Italian War of 1859, her contribution was to indulge in crying fits and general comments such as: The Emperor

The Hungarian coronation was celebrated in the Matthias Church in Buda. The Prince-Bishop, János Simor, assisted by Minister-President Andrássy, placed the King's crown on the head of Franz Josef and the so-called "house crown" on the head of his wife; then homage was paid to the royal couple. County Andrássy stands in the foreground on the right.

should make peace as soon as possible. When the 1866 war was about to begin, her opinion was: "It really would be by the grace of God if the King of Prussia were to die suddenly."

The sole exception to her political abstinence was made when she turned her attention to Hungary in the sixties. In 1849, the suppression of the Hungarian Revolt by the Austrians, with Russia's support, had been a bloody business and since then, as a punishment, the country

This picture shows Sisi wearing the Hungarian coronation robes. When Georg Raab painted it in 1867 he only had a few sketches and a series of photos to work from.

As a coronation present from the Hungarian people the Imperial couple were presented with Gödöllö Castle to the east of Budapest. This place soon became a great favourite of Sisi, and she was seen here more often than in Vienna – much to the irritation of the Viennese people.

had been governed centrally, from Vienna, as a part of Austria. The proud Hungarians, however, demanded back their old special laws, their constitution, their parliament and the crowning of Franz Josef as King of Hungary.

Mother-in-law Sophie hated the Magyars, whom she saw as dangerous rabble-rousers and trouble-makers. This was probably the most convincing reason for Elisabeth's Hungarian involvement. Moreover, she discovered that a "fellow feeling" existed between her and the people in the Puszta. "For her part, the Empress loved the Hungarians more than anything for their chivalrous character, predilection for riding and horses, fiery dances, soulful Gypsy ways and hot passionate nature, which was all so in keeping with her own feelings and nature." (E. Ketterl)

The shrewd Hungarians knew how to make the most of this affection, they flattered the Empress, enthusiastically praised her marvellous beauty, built up her opposition to the court, and placed a Hungarian companion, Ida von Ferenczy, in court circles around Elisabeth, as a secret agent, so to speak. She quickly became Sisi's closest friend and confidante and knew exactly how to bring the Empress round to the Hungarian way of thinking. Hungary soon became an idée fixe for the Empress, she became very enthusiastic about the national hero, Gyula Andrássy, immersed herself in learning Hungarian, sported Hungarian national costume, besieged her husband with requests to push ahead with the "compromise" with Hungary and every day, she wrote him long letters, intended as ultimatums: "I hope to hear, in the near future, that the Hungarian affair has finally been settled and that we shall soon be in the old fortress of Ofen. If you let me know that we can go, it will finally put my

mind at rest, as I shall know that I have achieved my heart's desire."

To start with, the Emperor put up a fight, but finally, swayed also by his advisers, he gave in and on June 8th, 1867, the Imperial couple were crowned King and Queen of Hungary. The grandiose celebrations lasted for five days. Sisi, quite out of character, participated tirelessly in all the balls and receptions. The Hungarian nation gave Sisi and Franz Josef the hunting lodge Gödöllö, which Sisi henceforth regarded as her real home, spending far more time there than in Vienna.

Sisi was proud, considered herself to be the saviour of the Hungarians and repaid Franz Josef for his compliance with marital affection. Ten months after the coronation, her daughter Marie Valerie was born, and not without making the most of the opportunity to provoke Vienna – the birth took place in Budapest.

 *Sport Can Kill You*

"Whenever she came to see us at Ischl, she always had at least forty horses with her," explained the Imperial villa guide to the public. "And here, between these two mirrors, she took charge of their morning exercises. She was so sporty, you see."

Sisi really was extremely sporty, especially when it came to riding. Even as a child in Possenhofen, she was a keen rider, then, as the young Empress, in Vienna and later, in the seventies, at the high point of her riding career, in Hungary, England, Ireland and Normandy. Sewn into her dark blue, fur-trimmed riding costume, a low top hat on her head, she was not just an "unforgettably beautiful sight", but also very soon one of the best huntswomen in Europe. Riding was an obsession for her, it was here that she

found her self-affirmation. "She has the knack of establishing an immediate, almost mesmeric relationship with her horse. She puts every other woman rider I know in the shade", certified a Viennese riding instructor. Clara Tschudi tells us, "Even the most malicious horses liked her to give them a smack. [...] She jumped the highest hedges without the least hesitation. When hunting, she usually easily cleared obstacles that brought even intrepid riders to a halt. She virtually frightened the director of the riding school in Vienna to death, by demanding that he give her the most uncontrollable animals in his possession. Often the horse beneath her fell and she was hurt, but this sort of accident was not able to diminish her passion for riding."

This didn't happen until 1882. That was when she suddenly stopped riding. We do not really know why. Was it because her master of the hunt, Bay Middleton had married and she was offended? Or was it her gout and her rheumatism, that spoilt her enjoyment? In any case, from this

In 1879 and 1880 the Empress won much praise in Ireland for her skills as a huntswoman. She remained little concerned about warnings that her Irish activities were perhaps politically rather inopportune and, in view of relations with England, ought better to be discontinued.

Hunting in England. Sisi (riding side-saddle!) and her trusted riding companion, Captain Bay Middleton, jumping over a hedge. The bearded man in the foreground is the host, Lord Harrington.

Sisi was also known in riding circles for her skill in dressage. Here we see her (1876) practising in the courtyard of Gödöllö Castle. Her horse was called Avolo and the painter of this piece, Wilhelm Richter.

Previous double page:

Sisi rode in Hungary, in England and in Ireland. In 1875 she stayed in Normandy, to prepare herself for the hunting season in England. Officially she was by the coast to accompany her daughter Valerie who was in urgent need of a sea-air cure.

Everywhere she lived Sisi had a gymnasium installed. Here we see her fitness studio in the Hofburg in Vienna – but unfortunately without the Empress; she never allowed herself to be photographed, not even by Mr Angerer, while performing her daily exercises at the rings, the wall bars, on the parallel bars and using the dumb-bells.

time on, she was seldom seen in the saddle.

But there had to be sport, sport keeps you beautiful, young and supple. "Elisabeth had blind faith in the power of sport to keep the body healthy and strong." (C. Tschudi), a thought that is not that far wrong, but does, however, require sport to be pursued with a modicum of good sense and not combined with starvation diets. But this is exactly what Elisabeth did and also exactly how quite a few of her illnesses can be explained. Sport and anorexia are not particularly happy companions. Doctors, who wanted to persuade her to eat sensibly and take more moderate exercise, were not given a hearing. "Really!" said the Empress to her daughter Valerie, "doctors and priests are such fools."

She exercised for hours in all the castles she lived in, and even in the Hotel Strauch in Feldafing an exercise room had to be set up for her. Then she started to fence – sabre, épée and foil. Of course, tradition insists that it was not long before her fencing masters were having to take great pains to avoid being run through and cut in two, but quite such spectacular successes obviously were not apparent here. In one of her poems, she portrayed the difficulties of a fencing lesson:

Dann kamst du, Säbel, an die Reih' / Mit deiner schartdurchwetzten Schneid', / Und schwer warst du, bei meiner Treu, / Mir deucht, mein Arm zeigt es noch heut'.
Die untern Hiebe, mein Malheur, / Die bracht' ich nimmermehr zustand; / Sie kamen stets zu plump und schwer / Aus meiner ungelenken Hand.

(Then it was your turn, sabre / With your much-dented blade, / You were heavy, as well, I must say, / It seems to me that my arm still feels it today. The low cuts, my little problem, / I could not get them right; / They were always too awkward, too heavy / When coming from my clumsy hand.)

A further Sisi sports poem was written in 1885:

Im Mondenschein, in Sonnenhitz / Bis zu der höchsten Felsenspitz / Steig' täglich ich hinan. / Ob's donnert auch und stürmt und blitzt, / Ob droben grauer Nebel sitzt, / Was liegt mir wohl daran!

(In the moonlight, in the heat of the sun / Right up to the top of the rock / I climb every day. / There can be thunder, storms and lightning, / The grey fog can lie in wait, / It makes no difference to me.)

Nothing mattered to her, she had now devoted herself to walking. Of course, she did not just go for a walk, like other people, she went for a run, for six, seven, eight-and-a-half, ten hours and became a jogger to be feared. "She really did run", one of her valets, Ketterl, tells us. "Her lady-in-waiting puffed and panted along beside her and a lackey brought up the rear. When the Empress picked up racing speed, she was throwing off clothing all the time. Now her cloak, now her jacket, then the shawl or the fur and the lackey had to pick up the individual items of clothing, as the Empress let them fall to the floor, and lug them around after her."

When the police saw her running, they often assumed that the ladies were being chased by a fiend and would rush in concerned pursuit, until they realised that it was Empress Sisi, hurrying along on a walk.

Where is the Empress?

Well, where is she then? Perhaps she is in Ischl, or in Bad Kissingen, for yet another cure? Or is she in Possenhofen? On the Riviera? In Corfu? Is she swimming in the cold North Sea? Or is she sitting on a horse at Towcester or Cottesbrook or somewhere else?

Or is she performing official duties, standing, with a sweet smile, at the side of the Emperor, in the presence of other

Elisabeth always had a fan with her, even when she was riding. She didn't need it to keep cool, but to hide her face when curious people or even photographers came across her. Which meant that cheeky photographers only managed to get shots such as this. Or ones in which she hid behind an umbrella.

Majesties, or in the presence of her people?

Because, "However much celebrations and court ceremony were not to the Empress's taste, she played her Imperial part for more than thirty years with inimitable grace and dignity. She moved freely among the people, went to the Prater, the park just outside Vienna and could always be seen at the opera, in the theatres and at concerts." (A. de Burgh)

"Always at the opera", sounds rather ironical. She was not even at the opening of the new opera house in May 1869. The architects had even designed a special room for her, with pictures of Lake Starnberg and of her favourite fairy queen, Titania, but urgent business prolonged her stay in Budapest. The celebrations were moved to a different date, when, although she was staying in Vienna, she was once again unable to attend. She was indisposed, a situation which so often seemed to crop up when she was attending to her official duties, just as it did for her royal Bavarian cousin, Ludwig.

"The Catholic church invites the Imperial household to be present on the occasion of the religious processions for Easter Saturday and the Feast of Corpus Christi. Every year, the Viennese looked forward to this magnificent sight. They looked forward to seeing the Empress at the head of the procession, followed by the ladies-in-waiting and the pages, carrying her train. But, invariably, a few days before the festival, they were informed that her Majesty had suddenly been taken ill and had travelled to the country, to recuperate." (C. Tschudi)

The Viennese were not impressed by this behaviour.

"Gradually, on those occasions when she was seen in public, her welcome became slightly less enthusiastic. People said she was proud and cold. It cannot be denied that she really taxed the patience of the Viennese, by appearing to be so indifferent to them. [...] Perhaps she herself was the first to feel that as far as both the middle classes in Austria and the higher social classes were concerned, she was no longer popular. This situation only served to increase still further her inclination to withdraw from the world."

Basically, however, nothing really dreadful was expected of her. Just her kind attendance, a gracious nod of her lovely head, a friendly expression. But unsociable Sisi had little desire to do this. She considered herself to be a private, even if highly important, individual. "What is the point in being Empress nowadays?" she asked her lady-in-waiting, Wallersee, "One is merely a dressed-up doll."

Quite apart from that, occasions of the official sort disturbed her day most appreciably. The day began in winter, at about six and in summer, as early as five, with a cold bath and a massage. This was followed by morning exercises, a meagre breakfast and then three hours of hair care and two to three hours of dressing and lacing up. A frugal midday meal was followed by riding or fencing instruction, then a walk, once again having her hair done, getting changed and at seven in the evening, if it really could not be avoided, a rapid family dinner, a brief conversation with the Emperor, for they didn't have much to say to each other anyway, and the day was at an end. As you can see, there was hardly room for a public smile in all this.

Now and then, however, she did have to show herself. Then she liked to hide herself behind a fan, for her beauty was her personal private property and did not concern anyone else. She gave "the impression that she was bored and deaf and dumb" and put on a gloomy expression, as

Sisi often visited the Isle of Wight. Queen Victoria used to spend her summers there, in Osborne House near Cowes, away from all the people. Nowadays ordinary folk can even visit Queen Victoria's private rooms. The island is dotted with picturesque little villages; this photo shows Winkle Street in Calbourne.

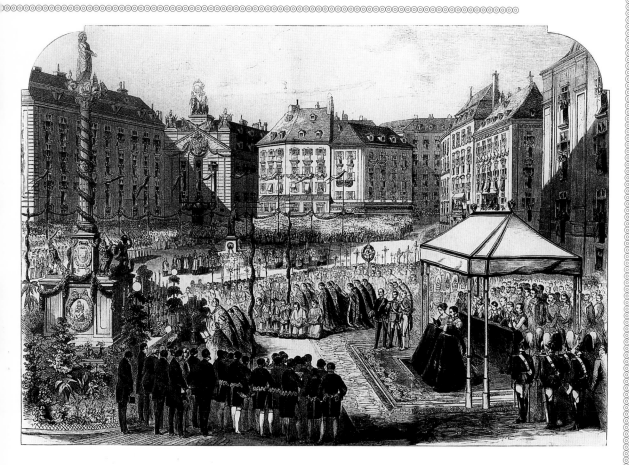

When a Corpus Christi procession or similar festive occasion took place in Vienna, Elisabeth was generally out of sorts or just happened to be away, which prevented her from taking part. Here we see her, praying devotedly, next to the Emperor on Lady Day. That was in July 1855, when she was not yet so skilled in the art of contracting sudden ailments.

Frau Wallersee tells us, "like an Indian widow, who is to be burned". 1873 was the best year for appearances. She visited the Holy Sepulchre in Vienna where, to the amazement of the pious population, she took part in the procession to mark the Feast of Corpus Christi. She made a brief appearance at the World Exhibition and in December, even interrupted her stay in Hungary for two days to join in at least part of the festivities to celebrate the silver jubilee of Franz Josef's reign. Although she did wear a heavy gauze veil in front of her face, so that no-one could see her.

In 1887, when staying on the Isle of Wight, she decided, at the request of the Emperor, to pay a visit to Queen Victoria. She then described what happened during the visit, in angry verse:

*Der Herrsch'rin dieses Inselreiches / Ihr soll heut'
gelten mein Besuch, / Als hätten wir an Langweil
gleiches / Nicht schon an unserm Hof genug. / Mit
Möven segeln um die Wette / Im Sturmgebraus, ist
Hochgenuss; / Doch hier die steife Etiquette, / Die
macht Titania nur Verdruss.*

(Ruler of this island kingdom / My visit today is meant for you, / As if we did not have already have / Enough of such boredom in our own court. / To race the seagulls / In the height of the storm, is high delight; / But here, rigid etiquette, / Only makes Titania frustrated.)

(By Titania, she means herself. Franz Josef appeared in her poems as Oberon, the King of the Elves.)

*Die Phrasen sind's, die altbekannten, / Man findet
sie in allen Landen: / »Wie geht's dem teuern Herrn
Gemahl?« / »O bestens lässt er sich empfehlen, /
(Wollt' er mich doch mit ihr nicht quälen!) / So
schrieb er aus dem Alpenthal.«*

(It's those old familiar phrases, / Every country has them: / "And how is your dear husband?" / "He's fine, he sends his regards, / [For did the imposition of her not come from him?] / He wrote from his Alpine valley.")

Devoted to the People

It is enjoyable and uplifting to leaf through the works of earlier Elisabeth biographers, who saw it as a pressing engagement to praise the wonderful perfection of the Empress beyond all measure. They intervened zealously with the correcting pen, even telling white lies, where necessary, should a disturbing flaw appear that could mar the pure portrait, or even sully it.

As is only proper for the noble shining lights of history, Empress Elisabeth was also praised for her countless, lovable deeds, which convince us that she had a big heart as far as her people were concerned, especially for the poor and that she never hesitated to intervene graciously, helpfully, genially and open-handedly, when need arose. A whole collection of sagas and legends, portraying these wonderful compassionate and charitable acts have grown up around the Empress, "who, herself a silent sufferer, feels so personally the sufferings of her fellow human beings" (A. de Burgh), knowing as she did "no politics other than to carry out good deeds and improve her surroundings" (L. Smolle).

Even as a child, this was how she behaved. "As she did not have much pocket money to buy presents, often in the evenings, she would knit stockings or make other items of clothing for her friends in the mountains." (C. Tschudi)

"In general, everywhere the Empress stayed, whether for a long or short time, she was praised and honoured as a saint, because of the many good deeds she performed for the poor people." (L. Smolle)

Later, on Corfu, she rowed out, single-handedly, to a hermit's island, with baskets of provisions and took personal charge of the restoration of a hut, so that a frail, gout-ridden old woman would not have to starve in a workhouse. Or in Norfolk, where "a wallet containing 400 pounds sterling" was handed over to the widow of a worker who was killed in an accident.

And is it not heartwarming to learn, as Conte Corti tells us, how she once saved a child from getting wet? "In the afternoon, Elisabeth went for a walk in the pouring rain, umbrella in hand. She saw a little girl, dressed only in thin clothes, shivering with cold. She laid a shawl over her shoulders, gave her the umbrella and said, 'There we are, it's a present', and went home through the downpour."

In 1993, a somewhat angry Professor Schilke brought harsh charges against her for her lack of social consciousness. "Fighting poverty in far-flung areas of the population was as uninteresting to her as equal rights for women, the promotion of social institutions such as hospitals, schools or homes. She was not in the least interested in improving the income position and the working conditions of large families living below the poverty line. The Empress did not see the distress in many of the regions of her realm and did not know how to handle the serious problems experienced by a multinational state. She ignored the desperate economic conditions of the rural population, the exploited industrial workers in the towns and the widespread use of child labour."

We would far rather read the opposite, as told to us by Clara Tschudi. "In the entire Hapsburg Empire, both in Austria and Hungary, there is hardly a single charitable institution or foundation which she has not protected or supported."

It has been verified that during the wars of 1859 and 1866, she visited the wounded

Previous double page:

Visits to hospitals, old people's homes and other institutions were not exactly to her liking but could not be avoided. Here she visited a soup kitchen for poor people, a scene which was captured in a painting by August Mansfeld.

She most liked to carry out her social responsibilities in lunatic asylums, such as here in the one on Leopoldsfeld in Budapest. Accompanied by her lady-in-waiting, Countess Festetics, she watched a hypnosis session here, and the "Interessante Blatt" (Interesting News) reported the occasion in detail.

and gave them cigars and that she called in to the lunatic asylums with great interest. It is also true that later on, her interest in this kind of visit waned. Even Frau Tschudi is not totally in agreement with her here.

"But as Elisabeth's predilection for a secluded life became ever more pronounced, quite understandably her predilection for involvement in public charity could not be strengthened. In later years, she only visited the public foundations in Austria, if pressurized by the Emperor. Neither did she have the patience to do this regularly. She accomplished her more official acts of mercy from behind a curious mask of coldness and haste, as if she were very pressed for time. When every so often, she turned up in the philanthropic establishments in Vienna, she arrived like a whirlwind, quite unexpectedly. On a single day she would make eight to ten such visits to the four corners of the capital, just as if she wanted to make good what she had neglected when she had not been there, as if she wanted to absolve her compassionate duties all in one go."

However, if we read on, we are pleased to note that things were not quite what they seemed.

"But she was a good woman. Up until her death, she supported numerous poor and needy souls. Even in Vienna, she sought out the wretched holes of suffering, unrecognised, even if not as frequently as in Budapest. But in general, the Viennese knew nothing about these acts of kindness, which she carried out in secret. It never occurred to them that the kind-hearted lady, who inundated her needy souls with good deeds, was the proud Empress, who was regarded as heartless by high and low alike and who was notorious for her indifference to the needs of others."

Elisabeth had four children: Sophie, who died young, Gisela and Rudolf, whom she could not stand, and Valerie (photo), who was born in 1868 and on whom she poured a suffocating love. In 1874, at the age of 37 she became a grandmother, and in 1895, at 58, a great-grandmother.

Children are the Bane of a Woman's Life

And how did she behave towards her children? Was she, as may be expected of such a charitable person, a loving mother, full of tender care?

To find out, let us turn once more to her biographer, de Burgh. He is quite moved by Sisi's wondrous maternal solicitude:

"Her Majesty the Empress fulfilled her motherly duties with true devotion. As heaven had blessed the Imperial couple with the births of a son and two daughters in the first years of their marriage, their family life was of the happiest. For many

Sisi in 1862 with dog, children and husband, who, here without uniform, is almost unrecognisable. Sisi thought that in ordinary dress he looked like "a shoemaker in Sunday best".

The Imperial/Royal family in Gödöllö. From the left: Crown Prince Rudolf, the Emperor and Sisi with Gisela and the favourite, Valerie. The lithograph from 1871 was by Vizenz Katzler.

years the Empress spent her free time either in the children's nursery with her cherished little ones, or in places where poverty and wretchedness might be alleviated. Her happiest days were those spent with her children in a mountain palace or a villa in the forest."

However, this version did not prove easy to sustain. Each of her subjects knew of Elisabeth's highly infrequent attendance at the children's nursery, so that the

school inspector, Herr Smolle (1904), felt obliged to make embarrassed excuses for her: "It is truly painful to the Empress that the duties imposed by her exalted position do not allow her to devote herself as fully as she would dearly wish to the upbringing of her charming little daughter, who is growing up with such grace."

But it was not like that either. She paid little attention to Sophie, Gisela and Ru-

Mayerling. Rudolf's hunting lodge, which used to stand on this spot, was demolished on the orders of the Emperor, after the death of the Crown Prince. It was replaced by a Carmelite monastery and has become a much-visited place of remembrance.

dolf. She later complained frequently and at length that her children had been estranged from her on purpose. Hardly were they born than her mother-in-law took them under her harsh protection. The "Imperial and Royal Nursery" was installed in Sophie's apartment; the Archduchess took over their education, appointed the wet-nurses, governesses and other personnel; Sisi was never asked and had no say in anything. "I was only allowed to see the children when Archduchess Sophie gave permission," she told Countess Festetics. "In the end I gave up the struggle and hardly ever went to see them."

We may assume that the children were looked after far better by their grandmother than by their nervy, capricious and irritable mother, who had little idea what to do with them and after their births was mainly concerned with regaining her slender figure by means of starvation diets.

Sisi, we are told, had a far warmer relationship to her dogs and horses than to her children, had a low opinion of both Gisela and Rudolf, and did not change her mind even when she became a grandmother and – in 1895 – a great-grandmother. She wrote of Gisela's second child: "Gisela's child is uncommonly ugly but very lively. It looks just like Gisela."

A lady-in-waiting, Maria Wallersee, quotes a saying of Sisi's: "Children are the bane of a woman's life, for they ruin her beauty." Which did not apply to Sisi: her

On 30 January 1889 Crown Prince Rudolf shot first his seventeen-year-old girlfriend, Marie Vetsere, and then himself. But what was the reason – illness or political difficulties? To this day it has remained unclear.

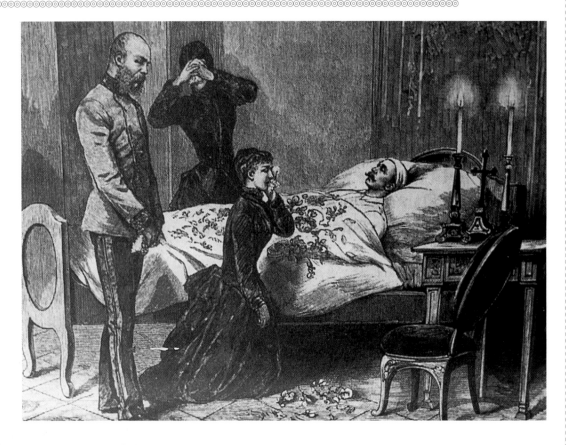

Franz Josef, Elisabeth and Rudolf's widow Stephanie at the death bed of the Crown Prince in the Hofburg in Vienna. The Empress, who cared little for her son when he was alive, sank into deep mourning after his death, and from then on always wore black.

beauty was said to have been actually enhanced by her pregnancies.

When she finally succeeded – more out of spite than affection – in having the children's nursery moved to her own apartments, she made little use of her newly-won maternal rights.

Her act of greatest motherly devotion came in August 1865, when she heard about the unduly harsh educational regime to which the Crown Prince was being subjected as a cadet. She now showed an energetic streak, insisting that the Prince's tutor be dismissed.

She experienced truly heartfelt motherly love only after the birth of her fourth child, Marie Valerie, who was born in 1868, much later than her other offspring. She was the only one of her children that she really loved, and who now had to endure all the tenderness which had been withheld from the others. This got on the nerves not only of those around her, but

of her daughter herself. "Mama's great love," Valerie said later, "weighs on me like a guilt that can never be atoned."

While her son Rudolf admired her, she for her part thought little of him. Only the tragedy at Mayerling, when Rudolf shot his mistress Marie Vetsera and then himself, awakened feelings for him, too – overpowering posthumous pangs of love that she could never shake off. Withdrawing into herself still more than before, for the rest of her life she wore only black clothes to signify her grief.

Twenty Five Years are Enough

The Imperial silver wedding anniversary fell on 23 April 1879. The populace flocked to Vienna, lined the streets, sang the Imperial anthem in stentorian tones and even Sisi, by now the "most beautiful grandmo-

In April 1879 Franz Josef and Elisabeth celebrated their silver wedding. A splendid procession was held through the middle of Vienna. Here on the square in front of the outer castle walls was a festival tent, to which were adjoined two glazed pavilions.

ther", made an appearance. On the eve of the celebration, the many archdukes and archduchesses performed tableaux vivants portraying historical scenes from the time of Rudolph I to Maria Theresa. The next day was devoted to worship; the Votivkirche was consecrated and a Haydn Mass performed by the male-voice choral society. Then, unfortunately, it rained, so that the main attraction had to be postponed until the 27th. This was the grand and wonderful "illustrated historical procession" put on by the citizens of Vienna in honour of the Imperial couple.

14,000 men and women took part; in fine historical costumes they portrayed the crafts, industry, trade, business, the railways, the fine arts and folklore. There were 230,000 spectators; for two hours the procession rolled past the Emperor and his Consort. "For almost this entire time the Emperor stood erect, fixing his gaze with utmost interest on the colourful pageant whose splendour no words can describe." (L. Smolle) Groups on horseback were followed by horn and trumpet players blowing fanfares; then came the displays, from the "painters and lacquer

The silver wedding couple. Sisi does not look particularly happy. She did not feel her 25 years of marriage to have been very happy – quite apart from the fact that this picture is probably a photomontage in any case – the image of Sisi, appropriately "aged" by the retoucher, was skilfully inserted into the arm of the Emperor.

The Festival Committee's programme for the procession through Vienna in honour of the silver wedding of their Imperial Majesties listed the order of the floats decorated by the various clubs and trade associations.

workers", the "brandy, risoglio and liqueur distillers", the "designers of ornamental and pleasure gardens", the "dyers of coloured and black cloths" to the pastrycooks, the "guilds on magnificent floats, with gigantic figures dressed in velvet and silk", and finally the group representing the fine arts, "the most dazzling of all, greeted with endless jubilant cries", with the painter Hans Makart at their head. He, "whose brush so delighted in glowing colours, had produced the designs for the different groups. A piece of the colourful Middle Ages had been set down in the sober present day." The people thanked him enthusiastically. "The artist's face, framed by his black beard, was pale with excitement, but the eyes of this man of genius, whose fantasies had come to life so splendidly, were radiant with joy. Wherever the dark rider appeared on his white palfrey, he was pointed out and the cry 'Long live Makart' went through the ranks." That is how the newspaper, the Neue Freie Presse, described the event.

The citizens of Vienna rejoiced, clapped and cried: "Hail Franz Josef! Hail Elisa!"

at the top of their voices. The Emperor was "deeply moved", while Sisi's emotion was "no less heartfelt".

However, she confessed to her niece Maria Wallersee that twenty-five years of marriage were enough, and that to put on festivities to celebrate them was superfluous. The silver wedding, she said, was not really a good reason for rejoicing, and had not the people of Vienna enjoyed the festival so much, she could have very well have done without it.

Sisi explained what she thought of marriage itself to her daughter Valerie in 1889. It was, she declared, "a perverse institution. One is sold off as a fifteen-year child, making a vow one does not understand, that one repents for the next thirty years or more, but cannot break." What was there to celebrate in that?

In August 1865, provoked by some dispute with the Emperor, she let him have it in writing: "I wish to retain unrestricted authority in all matters concerning the children, the choice of their surroundings, the place where they live, the full supervision of their education; in a word, I alone decide everything until they come of age.

I wish, furthermore, to have sole power of decision in all that concerns my personal affairs, including the choice of my entourage, my place of residence and all my domestic arrangements. Elisabeth."

With this ultimatum she had defined her position and declared her independence.

Somehow, the love she had once felt for Franz Josef had died. She mourned the fact in lyrical flights:

Wo ist der Schlüssel hingekommen? / Ich sucht' ihn ewig nicht hervor, / Den du zu meinem Herz genommen, / Der ging dir längst schon in Verlor!

(What has become of the key to my heart, / Which you have taken from me? / Endlessly have I looked for it, / But you lost it long ago.)

And was greatly surprised when, nevertheless, the Emperor knocked at her door:

Unsrer Liebe starre Leiche / Kamst du wieder zu beschau'n; / Und doch muss die kalte, bleiche / Tote dich im Innern grau'n.

(You came to gaze once more / On our love's rigid corpse; / Yet what horror must you have felt / To see that body, pallid and cold.)

For a long time now she had shown her husband only polite indifference and bored sympathy. And often not even that. "The Empress did not behave in an overly amiable way towards the Emperor; indeed, it seemed to be her intention to wound his feelings in every possible way. But Franz Josef always treated her with utmost chivalry. When she was staying in Vienna he sent a messenger to her every few hours, to enquire how she was," his valet, Ketterl, recalled. Gone for ever was his "sweet Sisi". "In Gödöllö he caught sight of his spouse only rarely, even when they were living under the same roof. If Franz Josef wanted to visit her in the morning and arrived without being announced, the servants told him that Her Majesty the Empress was still asleep.

Sometimes the great lady had already left for the mountains, and did not return with her unfortunate lady-in-waiting until the evening. And then, dog tired, she was even less inclined to receive the Emperor. So it often happened that the Emperor went to her in vain for ten days in a row. Anyone can imagine how embarrassing this was for him in front of the staff; often I felt really sorry for the great lord."

Lass' mich allein, lass' mich allein, / Für mich ist's jetzt das Beste; / Das Ganze kann's doch nie mehr sein; / Zu wenig sind mir Reste.

(Leave me alone, leave me alone, / That is best for me now; / We can never have it all again; / And all else is too little.)

Thus she addressed the Emperor, who accepted the rebuff with a humble devotion and a pleading subservience which showed clear traits of masochism. "Think now and then," he wrote to his "angelic Sisi", "of your sad and lonely little boy, who loves you so endlessly."

Sisi found this attitude entirely appropriate, acknowledging it in suitable verses:

Schliesslich warst du das treue Tier / Und liebst mich noch zur Stunde.

(You, after all, were the loyal beast Loving me even now.)

Tours for the Over-Fifties

If, earlier, Elisabeth had usually justified her absences from the Court and from Vienna by her somewhat idiosyncratic illnesses, now it was her deep, unending grief for her unloved son which made her wander the world like a black spectre.

The Emperor no longer mattered, her poetry dried up, not much of her beauty was left, her faced was lined, her feet were swollen and she was plagued by sciatica.

The Villa Hermes – so called after the Hermes statue standing in front of it – was built by the Emperor in the 1880s as a summer residence for Sisi, in the hope that she may stay a while in Vienna. The hope was a forlorn one. She never stayed longer than a few days here. Nowadays the villa is used for exhibitions.

Elisabeth's sumptuous bed-room in the Villa Hermes was designed by Makart. The wall paintings show scenes from Shakespeare's Midsummer Night's Dream. But it was all in vain, because the Empress preferred to continue her travels abroad.

On the island of Corfu Elisabeth had the Achilleion built. But, in 1891 when it was finished, she had already lost interest. In 1898 Gisela inherited it, and in 1907 it was acquired by Emperor Wilhelm II. Later it was taken over by the Greek government who set up two commemorative rooms to the Imperial Majesties, and also a casino (now transferred to the Corfu Hilton).

Achilles was Sisi's favourite hero, because he "despised all kings and traditions and considered the hordes of people worthless", and "only lived for his dreams". She named her Greek house after him. The photo shows the statue of the "Dying Achilles" by the Berlin sculptor, Ernst Herter.

In 1890 Count Andrássy died, her sister Helene died, and her favourite daughter Marie Valerie was married. What was left for her, a bored woman in her mid fifties with nothing to do?

She travelled, even more inordinately than before, rushing across Europe restlessly and aimlessly, to Gödöllö and the Côte d'Azur, to Naples and Sorrento, to Corfu, Holland, Ireland, England, Switzerland, Paris, Biarritz, Bad Kissingen, Dresden, Algiers, Spain and Portugal. "I wish to wander through the entire world," she declared, "Ahasuerus will be a stay-at-home compared to me. I wish to cross the oceans back and forth, a female Flying Dutchman."

Attempts to encourage a more sedentary lifestyle failed. The Villa Hermes in the zoological garden at Lainz, which the Emperor had had built for her between 1882 and 1886 at a cost of millions, she oc-

The salon carriage in the Empress's private train. It was a very comfortable way to travel through Europe. The carriage, built in 1873, is now in the Technical Museum in Vienna.

Miramare Castle on the Adriatic to the north of Trieste near Grignano. Built by Franz Josef's younger brother Ferdinand Maximilian, who became Emperor of Mexico in 1864 and was shot dead in 1867. The Emperor inherited the castle from his brother. Sisi often stayed here.

cupied for only a few weeks in a year. The Achilleion on Corfu, for which she had shown such enthusiasm, ceased to please her almost as soon as it was finished; by 1893 she was looking for a rich American to buy it from her.

Wherever she went, she found life unbearable:

*Eine Möve bin ich von keinem Land
Meine Heimat nenne ich keinen Strand,
Mich bindet nicht Ort und nicht Stelle;
Ich fliege von Welle zu Welle.*

(A seagull am I without a land
Or any shore to call my home.
No place can hold me fast
As I fly from wave to wave.)

She did not travel because she had any overwhelming desire to be in Aix-les-Bains, Caux, Lisbon, Barcelona, Corsica, on Lake Como, or in Milan or Genoa. On the contrary, she told her Greek tutor Christomanos: "My destinations are only desirable because of the journey before I get there."

Sisi's travels, on imperial yachts and in luxurious railway carriages, with her royal household, milk-cows and goats, her stays with her entourage in palaces and dignified Grand Hotels, were far from cheap. But that did not matter. The Empress had money enough. To begin with she had an annual appanage of 100,000 gulden; from 1875, when ex-Emperor Ferdinand died, leaving his enormous fortune to Franz Josef, she had 300,000 gulden annually at her disposal. And the Emperor paid her major expenses in any case.

The press observed her activities with a lively interest, and in newspapers published outside Austria the question was sometimes raised whether the Empress might not be suffering from a mental dis-

This picture was taken in 1894, when Elisabeth was 57 years old. It shows the Empress, and to her left, her lady-in-waiting and reader, Ida von Ferenczy.

order. This suspicion was not entirely far-fetched, especially to those who heard how Elisabeth had herself lashed to the deck of her ship in heavy storms, like a latter-day Odysseus; or how she was in the habit, on her walks, of pushing her way without a word of explanation into any strange house that took her fancy (and from which she was sometimes ejected); how she declined to see impor-

tant royal personages who wanted to visit her on the grounds that she was not sure whether she would be at home on that precise day, while she, for her part, was wont to descend unannounced on the houses of the highest nobility.

Or when, in 1896, at the millennial celebration of the conquest of the territory of present-day Hungary by Hungarian tribes, she sat as if turned to stone beside the Emperor in the throne room. "Her long lashes are lowered; of her kind, lively eyes nothing is to be seen; she sits quite still, almost numb, as if she can see no-one and hear nothing. Her soul, oh, how far away her soul might abide. No movement, no glance gives a sign of her interest. With her sorrowful, pallid face she resembles a white statue. She carries her great mourning with her everywhere." (Kálmán Mikszáth). The German ambassador, Count

Eulenburg, who also witnessed the scene, was less impressed and summed up his thoughts more bluntly: the sombre, black-clad queen had looked to him like "an ink blot on a very fine, colourful painting".

The Corpulent Angel

An important question which has always occupied the minds of admirers of princely goings-on is: Who has deceived whom, and if so, with whom? To this we can reply: Sisi's father, Maximilian, deceived his wife Ludovika, habitually and constantly. Likewise Rudolf his wife Stephanie. Sisi's sister Mathilde had an affair with a Spanish grandee, and her sister Marie a child by an officer of the guard – and a papal one at that. Sisi's sister

Sophie, as the betrothed of King Ludwig, had a relationship with a photographer, and later, when married, with a Herr Doktor Glaser from Munich – by which event Sisi was inspired to write accusatory verses:

Deinem guten Herrn Gemahl / Hast die Treue du gekündigt, / Stiessest ihm ins Herz den Stahl; / Ja, du hast dich schwer versündigt

(With your good spouse / You have broken faith, / Plunging your blade into his heart; / Yes, you have sinned most grievously.)

With regard to the intimate life of the Empress herself, scholars have concluded that she can be reproached with nothing scandalous, and that contemporary gossip to the effect that she had been involved with her riding friends Nikolaus Esterházy and Bay Middleton, with King Ludwig, with her equerry Imre Hunyády on Madeira or her tutor Constantin Christomanos on Corfu, or even that the Hungarian Count Andrássy was the father of her daughter Marie Valerie, is dismissed as malicious and without foundation. Sisi is suspected far more of frigidity than of illicit passions, a suspicion reinforced, among other things, by one of her own poems:

Für mich keine Liebe, / Für mich keinen Wein; / Die eine macht übel, / Der andere macht spei'n.

(For me no love, / For me no wine. / The first makes me ill, / The second makes me sick.)

Matters were rather different in the case of Franz Josef who, heartfelt as his devotion to his Sisi might have been, was never an overly faithful husband. His biographers record a number of liaisons in the years 1859/60; then there was the railwayman's wife, Anna Nahowski (born in 1859) with whom he had a protracted relationship, and reputedly several children, between 1875 and 1889. The Emperor always behaved with noble generosity towards his lady friends, a character trait which earned the Nahowski family a fine park villa in Hietzing and considerable wealth. In March 1889 Anna, after signing a statement saying that "I hereby swear that I will at all times remain silent concerning my encounter with His Majesty", received a "gift" of 200,000 gulden.

Franz Josef had a long-standing relationship with Anna Nahowski (later to become the mother-in-law of Alban Berg).

The end of the relationship with Anna Nahowski overlapped slightly with the beginning of the era of Katharina Schratt, giving Anna an opportunity to complain to her high-born lover about his new liaison:

"It is on everybody's lips. In the inn 'Beim Lothringer' the actors from the Burgtheater were talking about it quite freely. You hear the same thing at the grocer's, the butcher's and on every public carriage [...]."

To which the Emperor lied outright: "Do not believe such silly gossip. Frau Schratt is a very respectable woman, and I can assure you that there is nothing but friendship between us." (F. Saathen)

Katharina Schratt (born in 1853 in Baden near Vienna), a popular actress of naive comic roles at the Burgtheater, was the most famous and the most permanent of the Emperor's lady friends. Contemporaries describe her as an "innocuous, good-hearted soul" and "so homely" (the Emperor's daughter Valerie), as a "sweet, delightful woman" (the valet Eugen Ketterl), as a "charming, simple woman" (Maria Wallersee), as well as "beautiful and stupid" (Count Hübner, the Austrian ambassador in Paris).

Katharina Schratt was thirty-three and the Emperor fifty-five when they met, the match obligingly made by the ever-solicitous Empress.

Maria von Wallersee, Sisi's niece and lady-in-waiting, tells us the following: "When travel fever overcame Elisabeth in 1885, her kind heart reproached her bitterly at the thought that the Emperor might be lonely in her absence. 'Do you not know of any trustworthy woman who could keep the Emperor company and who would not try to influence him?' she asked me one day. I named several ladies who would certainly have been only too happy to console the Imperial grass

widower. But Aunt Sisi rejected them all, and the matter was not mentioned again until one day she suddenly informed me that she had found what she sought in the actress Katharina Schratt."

A chance meeting was arranged without delay; the friendship began, took its course and lasted thirty years until Franz Josef's death in 1916. The Emperor adorned Katharina Schratt with jewels, paid for her wardrobe, her furniture, her gambling debts and her property, allocated her an annual appanage of 30,000 gulden from his private family funds (at that time a university professor earned about 3000 gulden per annum), despatched her husband as a vice-consul to Tunisia, wrote

nearly a thousand letters to her, in which he signed himself her "deeply loving, yearning Franz Josef", breakfasted, dined and chatted with her. As to what else passed between them, the world is still pondering the enigma. Kisses, at any rate, are documented in the Imperial letters, even though they are always indicated discreetly by "–". But was there not something more? Did he, or didn't he?

As for the Empress, she was quite happy with things the way they were.

She knew her Franz Josef to be well looked after, and acted as patroness of the relationship. "Your kindness and solicitude, and the attentions of my friend, are the only light in my melancholy life", her grateful husband wrote to her.

Sisi showed her liking for Frau Schratt ostentatiously, sending her presents, inviting her, appearing publicly with her husband and his lady friend in order to head off unseemly suspicions. The loyal Imperial valet Ketterl noted accordingly in his memoirs: "It is well known that Empress Elisabeth and Frau von Schratt were very fond of each other, and that Frau von Schratt accompanied them when Franz

Josef and Elisabeth were travelling together. The two ladies got on famously, kissing each other repeatedly [...]". Katharina Schratt, for her part, believed herself a "friend of the Empress" throughout her life. After all, neither she nor Eugen Ketterl were aware of the poems which Elisabeth was composing:

Dein dicker Engel kommt ja schon / In Sommer mit den Rosen. / Gedulde Dich, mein Oberon! / Und mach nicht solche Chosen!
Im Häuschen der Geranien, / Wo alles fein und glatt, / Dünkt sie sich gleich Titanien, / Die arme, dicke Schratt.

(Your corpulent angel comes to us / With summer and the roses. / Be patient now, my Oberon, / Avoid such indiscretions.
In the summerhouse decked with geraniums, / Where all is fine and neat, / She thinks herself Titania, / The poor fat actress Schratt.)

In imitation of Heine, she mocked the Emperor and his lady-friend:

Der König Wiswamitra / Kehrt heim von seiner Kuh, / O König Wiswamitra, / O welch' ein Ochs bist du.

(The good King Wiswamitra / Returns home from his cow. / My good king Wiswamitra, / O what an ox are you.)

Which shows that Elisabeth did not regard the couple's idyll with complete equanimity. And it leads straight on to the subject of our next chapter: "Sisi the Poetess".

All I Can Do Is Write

As a fifteen-year-old, love-lorn Princess and as a disappointed young Empress, Sisi bemoaned her troubles in expressive verse (see p. 40). In the following thirty years she renounced poetry, but in January 1885 after she had given up riding and was in search of a new occupation, she returned to it, spurred on by heaven:

The Emperor's friend even managed to have a street named after her, even though it was only a small one. The Katharina-Schratt-Strasse is on the edge of Bad Ischl, on the main road to Salzburg, near to the Villa Schratt, which today is a restaurant.

Katharina Schratt (her married name was Frau von Kiss) was 23 years younger than the Emperor. He found warmth and comfort with her, but the general public did not believe that the relationship was purely platonic. When, in 1909, Schratt's husband also died, rumours began to spread that the Emperor would secretly marry her. (This painting of Schratt is by Franz Matsch).

Das Pferd, dies irdisch Kleinod meiner Seele, / Durch höhre Mächte ward es mir vertauscht; / Es trat das Flügelross an seine Stelle, / Und meine Seele flog nun wie berauscht.

(The horse, this earthly jewel of my soul, / Was taken away from me by higher might; / In its place came the winged stallion, / And my soul now soared enraptured.)

Her soul was to spend four years in that rapture; between then and the winter of 1888/89 she wrote a whole book of poetry:

Wird mir die Welt zu bitter, / Die Menschen zu fatal, / So schwing' ich mich aufs Flügelross / Und mach' mich von der Erde los; / Ich flieh' die bösen Zwitter / Und die Canaillen all'.

(When the world seems too bitter, / And people too dire, / I swing into the saddle of my winged horse / And escape this earth; / I flee the ill-meant fickleness / And the whole canaille.)

Her poetic period ended with the suicide of the Crown Prince at Mayerling, she fell into silence.

Elisabeth considered herself to be a gifted lyricist and made complicated arrangements concerning how and where her manuscripts were best to be kept,

bis einst, nach wechselvollen Jahren / die Lieder blühend daraus aufersteh'n

(Until the time, when, after eventful years / The songs will rise up again in full glory).

Later, around the year 1950, after all the contemporaries had long since departed this earth, they were to be published for the benefit of the understanding "future spirits" of the world to come.

Elisabeth worshipped Heinrich Heine and wrote, "Every word, every letter, that appears in Heine is a jewel"; she claimed that Heine, with whom she was engaged in frequent spiritual contact, had written her poems:

Vom Abend bis zum Morgen, / Von Früh bis in die Nacht / Muss ich stets lauschen, horchen, / Ob du mir nichts gesagt.
Das Murmeln deiner Ebbe, / Das Rauschen deiner Flut / Das sind mir alles Worte, / Zu halten treu in Hut.
Mir dünkt, dass du dictiertest, / Zu schreiben nur bleibt mir; / Gedanken und Gefühle / Wehst du auf das Papier.

(From evening to morning, / From dawn to dusk / I listen, I hearken, / To hear what you say to me.
The murmuring of your ebb, / The roaring of your flood / These to me are all words, / For my faithful keeping.
It seems to me that you are dictating, / All I can do is write; / The thoughts and feelings / That you flutter onto the paper.)

Sisi, now in her mid-sixties, with her favourite dog, Shadow. A marble statue of this dog is to be found in the grounds of the Emperor's Villa in Ischl. Sisi liked to be photographed with her dogs, in preference to her husband and her children.

It seems quite evident, does it not, that poetic value is not the attraction in these verses; we can only hope that the Empress was wrong and that it was not Heine who fluttered these lines onto paper.

The significance of the Empress's verse goes far beyond the literary, and lies instead in the fact that these documents convey the convictions and thoughts, the opinions and sensitivities of Elisabeth (who otherwise left us very little in the way of writings); they give us insight into her opinion on the Imperial Court in Vienna and its personalities, and on the general social and political scene; they are an uncensored witness of her as a pacifist, anti-militarist, republican, virtual revolutionary, dreamer and illusionist.

She rejected the institution of monarchy and described it as "a bygone, glorious skeleton"; princely rulers ought to be abolished:

Wer weiss! gäb's keine Fürsten, / Gäb' es auch keinen Krieg; / Aus wär' das teure Dürsten / Nach Schlachten und nach Sieg.

(Who knows! If there were no princes, / There would be no wars; / That would be the end of the expensive thirst / For battles and for victory.)

And while she was about it, the whole parasitic aristocracy could go with them:

Besser waren auch die Fischer, / Ehrlich, arbeitsam und schlicht, / Als das Heer Aristokraten, / Das auf fauler Haut hier liegt.

(Even the fishermen were better, / Honest, hard-working and simple, / Better than the whole army of aristocrats, / That laze about here.)

Animals fared somewhat better:

Doch am höchsten muß ich schätzen, / Dass kein Tier vermag zu schwätzen, / Folglich auch zu lügen nicht; / Lügen thut nur, was auch spricht.

(But highly indeed do I prize, / The fact that animals are not disposed to chatter, / And therefore also not to lie; / For lies can only come from those that speak.)

She threatened her Hapsburg relations with:

In a small temple in the garden of the Achilleion on Corfu Elisabeth had a monument erected to Heinrich Heine. As soon as Emperor Wilhelm bought the villa he had the statue removed and replaced with a monument to Elisabeth. Heine's statue now stands in Toulon.

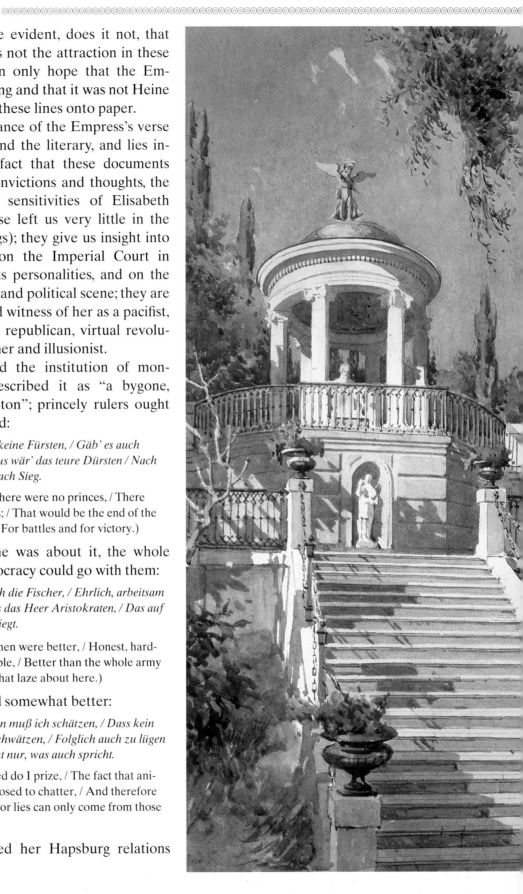

Ich aber web' euch Kappen / Und näh' auch Schellen dran; / Als Narren geht ihr dann herum, / Man schaut sich lachend nach euch um; / Und seid ihr längst begraben, / Sie klingeln selbst noch dann.

(But I will weave you caps / And even sew bells on them; / As fools you will then be attired, / People will look at you and laugh; / And even when you are long buried, / They will still be ringing.)

And she wickedly caricatured the participants in the Imperial family's Sunday meal:

Diese, einer Schweizer Kuh / Gleich an fetten Formen, / Dünkt sich doch in stolzer Ruh' / Schön bis zum Abnormen.
Jene aber, hässlich, wie / Eine Hex im Märchen, / Lässt am Nebenmenschen nie / Steh'n ein gutes Härchen.
Die in greller Pfauenpracht / Dort und falschem Zopfe, / Ei, wie sie sarkastisch lacht, / Mit dem schiefen Kopfe!

(This one, like a Swiss cow / With rounded forms, / Peaceful and proud, she thinks herself / Abnormally beautiful.
But that one, as ugly as / A witch in a fairy story, / Has never a good word / To say about other people.
And the one decorated like a peacock / With fake plaits, / Oh, what a sarcastic laugh, / And a crooked head!)

She called for rebellion against the House of Hapsburg:

Ihr lieben Völker im weiten Reich, / So ganz im Geheimen bewundre ich euch: / Da nährt ihr mit eurem Schweisse und Blut / Gutmütig diese verkommene Brut.

(You dear peoples in the wide empire, / I have secret admiration for you: / You good-naturedly feed with your sweat and blood / This rotten brood.)

She sang the praises of the North Sea and compared it to her own restlessness:

Wohl lieb' ich dich, du stolzes, / Du rauhes, barsches Meer / Mit deinen wilden Wogen, / Mit deinen Stürmen schwer!
Frei will ich dich umkreisen, / Wie deine Möven hier, / Ein bleibend' Nest zu bauen… / Für mich gibt's kein Revier.

(How I do love you, you proud, / You raw, brusque sea / With your wild waves, / With your mighty storms!

Supposedly one of the last photographs of Elisabeth, taken in 1898, several months before her death. However, it is more likely to be a photo-montage.

Elisabeth was worried that the Bavarian Prince-Regent would "have himself anointed King" but this in fact never happened. After the death of the Bavarian King Ludwig, his mentally ill brother Otto continued as King, with Prince Luitpold acting as Prince-Regent. This picture of Prince-Regent Luitpold, painted in 1902, is by Friedrich August von Kaulbach.

I want to circle freely above you, / Like your seagulls here, / And build a permanent nest … / For me there is no territory.)

She was less enamoured of the Suez Canal:

Die Flut im Suez-Kanale, / Die wälzt sich gelb und dick / Und spiegelt selbst nicht einmale / Das kleinste Blau zurück.

(The tide in the Suez Canal, / Wallows thick and yellow / And does not even reflect / The tiniest bit of blue.)

She complained of her loneliness:

Es teilt mein Seelenleben kein Gefährte, / Die Seele gab es nie, die mich verstand.

(No companion shares my spiritual life, / No soul ever understood me.)

Which is hardly surprising, because she was not like other people:

Wandle ich auch unter Menschen, / Ihresgleichen bin ich nicht.

(Though I may walk among other people, / I am not of their kind.)

She devoted thoughtful lines to the question of where the soul goes after death:

Doch wohin? ist die Frage, / Der grosse Hieroglyph, / Der Seele bittre Plage, / Das Rätsel, grundlos tief.

(Yet where to? Is the question, / The great hieroglyph, / The bitter torment of the soul, / A mystery of bottomless depth.)

She was concerned that the genes of Wittelsbach family madness could also reside in her, and, in a free adaptation of Heine's travel prose, takes up the cudgels for the confused:

Den Verrückten als Propheten / Ehren hoch die Orientalen; / Aber hier in diesem Lande / Müssen beide stürzen fallen.

(The Orientals hold in high honour / The crazy one as a prophet; / But here in this land / Both come tumbling down.)

She proclaims her daughter-in-law, Stephanie, to be a "mighty oaf" and a "toad, yellow and fat". Her own daughter fares no better; a verse from 1887 portrays her, sitting next to the Emperor, at a meal with her four children and husband, Prince Leopold of Bavaria, in the following words:

Oberon zu Deiner Linken / Einer rackerdürren Sau / Blaue Äuglein ehrlich blinken, / Ähnlich Dir fast im Geschau.
Ihre Ferklein, herzig kleine, / Bracht' sie aus dem Nachbarreich; / Sehen dort dem Vaterschweine / Bis aufs letzte Härchen gleich.

(Oberon, to your left / A rake-thin sow / Little blue eyes blinking honestly, / Quite like you in looks. Her tiny little piglets, / Brought with her from the neighbouring empire; / Look like their father pig / Right down to the last little bristle.)

She cursed the Bavarian Prince Luitpold as the main culprit in the death of King Ludwig. In this she shared popular opinion at the time:

Seht den heuchlerischen Alten! / Drückt ihn sein Gewissen nicht? / Thut so fromm die Hände falten, / Sauersüss ist sein Gesicht.
Wie sein langer Bocksbart wackelt! / Falsch're Augen sah man nie; / Ist sein Hirn auch ganz vernagelt, / Steckt es doch voll Perfidie.
Seinen Neffen, seinen König / Stiess er tückisch von dem Thron; / Doch dies ist ihm noch zu wenig, / Säh' sich dort gern selber schon.
Könnt ihr auch noch dies ertragen / Bayerns Volk, dann seid ihr's werth, / Dass, am Pranger angeschlagen, / Ihr in Ewigkeit entehrt!
Eh' sie ihn zum König salben, / Stürzt mit donnerndem Gekrach / Wenigstens ihr, stolze Alpen, / Tötend über Bayerns Schmach!

(See the hypocritical old man! / Does not his conscience trouble him? / Folding his hands so piously, / With his sweet and sour face.
How his long goat's beard wobbles! / Falser eyes were never seen; / Little wonder that his brain is so wooden, / For it is full of perfidy.

His nephew, his King / He ousted maliciously from the throne; / Yet even this is not enough, / For he wishes to see himself in that place.
But if you bear this too, / Bavarians, then you shall deserve, / To be dishonoured for eternity, / Beaten in the stocks!
Before they anoint him King, / At least you, proud Alps, / Will come thundering down, / To kill Bavaria's shame!)

Even the Swiss came in for some complaints:

Schweizer, Ihr Gebirg ist herrlich! / Ihre Uhren gehen gut; / Doch für uns ist sehr gefährlich / Ihre Königsmörderbrut.

(People of Switzerland, Your mountains are wonderful! / Your clocks all run to time; / But for us the biggest danger is / Your murderous royal brood.)

How right Sisi was! As was proven eleven years later.

Through a Tiny Opening into Heaven

On September 10th, 1898, on an otherwise pleasant, sunny day in early autumn, at about two in the afternoon, Empress Sisi/Elisabeth died, aged 60 years, eight months and seventeen days; the place was Geneva in the hotel "Beau-Rivage".

Sisi was in Switzerland to take the waters at Territet, and had been to visit Baroness Rothschild, staying overnight in the hotel "Beau-Rivage". She then left to return over Lake Geneva to Montreux. She was in a good mood and was chatting with her lady-in-waiting, Countess Sztáray, commenting on the beautiful chestnut trees, when suddenly a young man ran up to her, jostled with her and, unnoticed, stabbed a very finely sharpened file into her heart.

The Empress fell to the floor, but got up again, angrily rearranged her hat, was handed her umbrella and fan and addressed the assembled with, "I'm alright,"

The Empress was murdered by an assassin who stabbed a sharpened file into her heart. A small plaque at the site of the deed on the Quai du Mont-Blanc reminds the visitors to Geneva of the event.

Following double page:
Lake Geneva at Montreux. This is where Elisabeth was intending to take the ship over to Territet where she was staying for a rest cure.

Assassinat de l'Impératrice d'Autriche
LE CRIME

and asked, "What did that person want?". Then she called, "Let's hurry on board." She then walked over to the ship, "energetically" as was reported, went aboard, swooned but came to, asking, "What's happening to me?". She then collapsed again, was carried into the hotel and died.

It seems quite amazing that she was able to reach the boat, despite having been stabbed in the heart, but, as the doctors explained, the file was very thin and therefore the wound quite small. This meant that the blood only flowed slowly out of the heart, and it was a while before the heart stopped functioning.

What did that person want? – His name was Luigi Lucheni, 26 years old, born in

The "Freie Presse" reports that she was stabbed by Lucheni shortly after leaving the boat, whereas in fact it took place just before she went on board.

Paris and left in a spital there by his Italian mother; he grew up as an orphan, living in homes and hostels, and he worked as a labourer and cavalry soldier, officer's servant and bricklayer; he was an anarchist and had taken up the struggle against the mighty, the rich and the lazy. Only those who worked, he thought, should be allowed to eat. Death to the aristocracy!

It was pure chance, or just out of desperation, that he should have stabbed the Austrian Empress of all people (who in any case hardly ate anything and in fact shared his opinion). His actual victim was intended to be the Pretender to the Crown, Prince Henri of Orléans; but he wasn't there, and so he simply selected any other high-ranking person – it didn't matter to him whether that person was a king, president, prince or empress, and so his choice fell on Elisabeth.

Shortly after he was arrested and put on trial. He was proud of his act and of the fame it had brought him through the

After the deed the murderer Luigi Lucheni ran off, but was soon captured. Smiling broadly and mightily pleased with himself and what he had done, he is led away.

The Empress died in the Hotel Beau Rivage. A special detachment of the Swiss army came to collect the body. In a glass case in the reception of the hotel are Sisi's gloves, her hat and a few faded roses. Also two dresses that she left in the hotel are among the hotel's reliquaries.

newspapers. He was convicted and sentenced to life imprisonment; in 1910 he hanged himself in his cell.

The world was outraged, the Viennese beat up a few Italian building labourers and on September 17th Elisabeth was buried, in Vienna, in the Capucin Crypt.

Sisi's death was seen as tragic, horrible and terrible. But was it? Was it really so sad?

Wasn't it perhaps, in a way, a very beau-

tiful end that she met? Sudden and unexpected, unnoticed, quick, with no long-lasting infirmity, no intensive care, altogether quite satisfactory. Yet at the same time dramatic, and, when we forget that Sisi was really a substitute in this case, quite befitting her rank and status; it was aesthetically perfect, and aroused much sympathy. Who would not like to end their life in such a way, given that it must end – helped on their way into heaven by

War es ein Traum? — In einer jener Nächte,
Die unser Kaiser wachend zugebracht
Auf seiner Karte, folgend dem Gefechte
Der fernen beispiellosen Riesenschlacht —
Da stieg empor vor ihm in Strahlenhelle
Die Lichtgestalt, die — ach zu früh — entfloh'n,

Wenden!

the prayers and sympathy of half the world, and moreover, without really leaving any great vacuum?

Indeed, a treacherous murder was quite in keeping with the mood of a melancholic Empress, tired of life. "I yearn for death," she is supposed to have said, "I am ready to die. All that I wish is that I do not have to suffer too much or too long. I wish my death to be quick and painless. I do not want to die in my bed." (C. Tschudi) – "I would wish that my soul could slip through a tiny opening in my heart into heaven." (J. de la Faye) – And this is exactly what happened (but we can make no guarantee about heaven).

Of course, it is difficult to say how authentic these quotes are; the art of poetry is very quick and skilful in its retrospective on such cases. Yet even if the actual words are not true, then the sentiment and intention behind them certainly are.

This is how Elisabeth once looked to King Ludwig – wearing diamond jewels, slim, beautiful and young. And so she appeared to her war-waging Emperor-husband: "Victory, Emperor, victory – the enemy must be crushed / Courage to your brave sons!" she calls to him.

The Capucin Crypt in Vienna. Emperor Franz Josef lies buried here. Beside him is the sarcophagus of Crown-Prince Rudolf (left) and the Empress (right). Franz Josef died in 1916, at the age of 86. This brought him an entry in the Guinness Book of Records as the longest-reigning Austrian monarch.

A photograph of the Empress by Angerer, taken in 1867.

Sisi Bibliography - A Selection

Rosa Albach-Retty: So kurz sind hundert Jahre. Munich–Berlin 1978

Marie Blank-Eismann: Sissi. Der Schicksalsweg einer Kaiserin. Dresden 1937

Jean de Bourgoing: Briefe Kaiser Franz Josephs an Frau Katharina Schratt. Vienna–Munich 1964

A. de Burgh: Elisabeth, Kaiserin von Österreich und Königin von Ungarn. Blätter der Erinnerung. Vienna 1901

Raymond Chevrier: Sissi. Das Leben der Kaiserin Elisabeth von Österreich. Stuttgart 1987

Constantin Christomanos: Tagebuch-Blätter. Vienna 1899

Egon Caesar Conte Corti: Elisabeth. Die seltsame Frau. Graz–Vienna–Cologne 1934

Mary Cuncliffe Owen: The Martyrdom of an Empress. London 1903

Aloys Dreyer: Maximilian, Herzog in Bayern. Schriftsteller und Komponist. Munich–Leipzig 1919

Jacques de la Faye: Elisabeth von Bayern, Kaiserin von Österreich und Königin von Ungarn. Halle 1914

Francis Gribble: Franz Joseph. Berlin 1921

Brigitte Hamann: Sisis Familienalbum. Dortmund 1980

Brigitte Hamann: Kaiserin Elisabeth. Das poetische Tagebuch. Vienna 1984

Brigitte Hamann: "Meine liebe, gute Freundin!" Die Briefe Kaiser Franz Josephs an Katharina Schratt. Vienna 1992

Brigitte Hamann: Elisabeth, Kaiserin wider Willen. 14th ed. Vienna–Munich–Berlin 1995.

Joan Haslip: Elisabeth von Österreich. Munich 1972

Eugen Ketterl: Der alte Kaiser. Wie nur Einer ihn sah. Vienna–Munich–Zurich–Innsbruck 1980

E. M. Kronfeld: Franz Joseph I. Intimes und Persönliches. Vienna 1917

Museum Österreichischer Kultur, Eisenstadt: Elisabeth, Königin von Ungarn (Exhibition Catalogue). Vienna–Cologne–Weimar 1991

Friedrich Saathen: Anna Nahowski und Kaiser Franz Joseph. Aufzeichnungen. Vienna–Cologne–Graz 1986

Franz E. Schilke: Elisabeth und Ludwig II. Im Spiegel von Medizin und Kunst. Munich 1993

Leo Smolle: Elisabeth. Kaiserin von Österreich und Königin von Ungarn. Ein Lebensbild. Vienna 1904

Irma Gräfin Sztáray: Aus den letzten Jahren der Kaiserin Elisabeth. Vienna 1909

Clara Tschudi: Elisabeth, Kaiserin von Österreich und Königin von Ungarn. Leipzig 1906

F. B. Tschudy: Illustrirtes Gedenkbuch zur immerwährenden Erinnerung an die glorreiche Vermählungsfeier Seiner k. k. Apostolischen Majestät Franz Joseph von Oesterreich mit ihrer königl. Hoheit der Durchlauchtigsten Frau Herzogin Elisabeth in Baiern, vollzogen in Vienna am 24. April 1854. Vienna 1854

Juliane Vogel: Elisabeth von Österreich. Momente aus dem Leben einer Kunstfigur. Vienna 1992

Maria Freiin von Wallersee: Meine Vergangenheit. Wahrheit über Franz Josef / Schratt / Kaiserin Elisabeth / Andrassy / Kronprinz Rudolf / Vetschera. Berlin 1913

Maria Freiin von Wallersee: Kaiserin Elisabeth und ich. Leipzig 1935

Henri de Weindel: Behind the Scenes at the Court of Vienna. London 1914

John Welcome: Die Kaiserin hinter der Meute. Elisabeth von Österreich und Bay Middleton. Vienna–Berlin 1975

Photo Credits

(The location in which the photograph was taken is given in brackets, in cases where this is not identical with the photo source)

Alban Berg Stiftung, Vienna: 96

Archiv für Kunst und Geschichte, Berlin: 92, 94, 105

ARTOTHEK – Joachim Blauel, Peissenberg: 102 (Munich, Bayerische Staatsgemäldesammlungen)

Bayerische Staatsbibliothek, Munich: 21 bottom

Bayerische Verwaltung der staatlichen Schlösser, Gärten und Seen, Munich: 57 (Herrenchiemsee, Ludwig-II.-Museum)

Bildarchiv Bruckmann, Munich: 1 (Budapest, Magyar Nemzeti Muzéum), 52, 111

COLORVISION © Hans Rudolf Uthoff, Hamburg: 44/45, 91 top and bottom

IFA-BILDERTEAM: 6/7 (Lauer), 19 (Riedl)

Archiv/INTERFOTO, Munich: 22, 46, 54, 55, 56

Sammlung Jean Louis, Munich: 58, 59

Kunsthistorisches Museum, Vienna: Cover, 13, 47, 51, 63

Magyar Nemzeti Muzéum, Budapest: 62, 67 bottom, 81, 95

Ludwig Merkle, Munich: 29, 48, 60, 73, 98, 110 top

Ali Meyer, Historical & Fine Art Photography, Vienna: 2/3 (Vienna, Kunsthistorisches Museum), 4/5, 24/25 (Vienna, Kunsthistorisches Museum), 26 (Vienna, Hofburg), 31 (Vienna, Historisches Museum), 34/35 (Schloss Schönbrunn), 53, 70, 82, 83 (Vienna, Heeresgeschichtliches Museum), 87 (Vienna, Historisches Museum), 89, 90, 99 (Vienna, Historisches Museum), 108 top, 110 bottom

Münchner Stadtmuseum, Munich: 14 (© Wolfgang Pulfer), 16, 17 (© Wolfgang Pulfer), 21 top

Copyright by Direktion der Museen der Stadt Wien: 33, 36, 37 (Fotostudio Otto, Vienna), 76/77, 100, 101

Österreichische Nationalbibliothek, Vienna: 20, 23, 30, 38, 39 top, 41, 61, 67 top, 71, 74, 78, 80, 85, 86, 97, 103, 108 bottom

Private archive: 18, 79

© Ulli Seer/LOOK: 8/9, 43

Süddeutscher Verlag, Bilderdienst, Munich: 32, 84, 109

© Technisches Museum Vienna (Photo: E. Babsek): 93

Martin Thomas, Aachen: 68/69, 106/107

Fürst Thurn and Taxis Kunstsammlungen, Regensburg: 15, 49

Tourist board/Spa authorities, Bad Ischl (© Foto Hofer): 27, 28

© Viennaslide, Vienna: 64 (Harald A. Jahn), 66 (Wanzel)

Wittelsbacher Ausgleichsfonds, Munich: 50

© Ernst Wrba, Sulzbach/Taunus: 10/11, 39 bottom, 40